Journey to Woo Woo Land

Nicki Hughes

ISBN: 1500535435
ISBN 13: 9781500535438

GRATITUDE

In many books you will read the acknowledgments at the beginning, and it has taken me a long time to compile mine—so long that the book was almost ready to go to print and was delayed due to getting this absolutely right. I have never really paid much attention to this section in books I read, and it wasn't until I had to write my own that I saw how important it is for an author to show thanks and gratitude to those who have helped him or her along the way—even more so for me, as the book is all about journeys!

So I begin by thanking Christa Mackinnon, who has the most beautiful acknowledgments at the front of her book, *Shamanism and Spirituality in Therapeutic Practice.* A great inspiration! After a weekend retreat with Christa a few years ago, I really opened and developed my Shamanic roots, and with her encouragement, I understood the value of writing a book.

Together with connections I have made through Twitter over the past four years, I would like to show gratitude to Louise Hulland for enjoying my blog posts so much that she told me to write a book, together with Michael Wombat and Vivienne Tuffnell, who both encouraged me to opt for self-publishing. It would also be remiss of me to leave out the amazing Jane Alexander, who has also inspired me over the last few years, as has Ann-See Yeoh, who has encouraged me to develop my yoga from the feel and not the shape of the pose (and when I began to understand that, chapter ten was born!). Meanwhile I have Phil Steward, a fellow Reiki master, from Hands On in Braunton, to thank for chapter six. Another who has crossed my path is Louisa Miles, the catalyst for my move into social media, without whom I am sure this book would have been a lot longer in its evolution.

Heartfelt gratitude goes to my clients and students, without whom there would be no story, no growth, and no one to teach. There is Annabel Tempest, my friend and illustrator, who has been on a woo woo journey of her own while working on the illustrations for this book, and Ben Barnett, a real catalyst to my selling up and moving on, who I will always think of when the 'thinking outside the box' analogy pops up. There is no box. I know that now.

My lovely husband certainly deserves a mention, for without his help in the early stages of our marriage, we would never have been able to purchase our first salon, and the story would be a completely different one. He still thinks I'm a bit 'woo woo' but takes it with a pinch of salt and has always stood by me in everything I have wanted to do.

There have been many, many people who have met me along the path to offer guidance either knowingly or by silently dropping markers to light the way. To all who have done so, I am eternally grateful.

FOREWORD

It has been a long time coming, but apparently this is something I must do. Over the years I have written little nuggets of information and informative blog posts that have helped many people, and if I had a pound every time someone said, 'You should write a book'—well, I would have more money! I have finally taken the hint and written a book to put all the information in one place.

I am writing from the perspective of a normal person who is grounded and not away with the faeries all the time. Some would question, 'What is normal, anyway?' Apparently my writing makes sense. It's not too 'woo woo'. This is my term for people speaking from a very esoteric or spiritually 'energetic' point of view. As many of my friends will say when I talk about energies, pathways, therapies, and healing, 'Oh, she's off on one of her woo woo moments again.' These friends over the years have gradually begun to see where I'm coming from. They're not always converted—just more aware and much more connected.

So who am I? Who am I to be writing a book? Having spent twenty-six years in the field of holistic therapies, growing and emerging, teaching and treating, I feel I have a great deal to share. I first studied as a beauty therapist and hairdresser in the 1980s. In those days the words 'holistic' or 'spa' weren't even heard of; in fact, aromatherapy was labeled 'alternative medicine'. These types of therapies were not available to learn at college, and herbalism, homeopathy, Bowen therapy, etc., were labelled by most people as 'weird'.

After leaving college in 1987, qualified in hairdressing and beauty therapy, I rented a small room above a hairdressing salon in Taunton, which after two years enabled me to move to larger premises where I worked alongside my mother and stepfather for eleven years. During this time the 'spa' industry was born. Until then, the most indulgent treatment available was a salty body scrub followed by a massage. There were no body wraps or seaweed therapies. There were no self-tanning treatments or gel nails. My interest in treating the whole client, rather than just the symptoms, grew during the early 1990s, when a variety of people came into my path and enabled me to develop new skills. The industry as a whole grew very quickly in a short space of time. Not only did the 'beauty therapy' side become hi-tech with nonsurgical face-lifts, anticellulite machines, and oxygen facials, but the holistic side became more interesting to the 'normal' salon. This enabled therapies such as reflexology and Reiki to become part of many salons' service menus.

I married in 2000 and set up my own spa in the centre of Taunton. Genesis Day Spa was a dream come true, and I was able to introduce a more holistic approach to my team of therapists. Although not all beauty therapists have an interest in the holistic side, I was able to see who enjoyed the cosmetic treatments, such as manicures and makeup, and those who were desperate to work with the more subtle energies and healing side of the industry.

In 2003 I expanded, as my dream goal was to have five salons by the time I turned forty, brand them as a chain, and then sell them all. I opened a second salon in Ilminster, and during this time my interest in Reiki developed to a higher level. I became a Reiki master and started teaching others to be able to use energies in their daily life. It was during that time that my life path changed—one of those 'light bulb moments' that we hear about, a real defining moment during a treatment I was receiving myself.

My husband is military and has a saying: 'Plans are a basis for change.' This is a phrase that used to irritate me in our early days of marriage, as plans changing were often a disruption to my routine. However, as my life started to become more flexible, and I started to look into the more subtle energies and workings of the universe, I decided to draw the 'plans are a basis for change' card. I sold both salons. A big leap of faith, but I did it, and I now have a unique, purpose built holistic centre set in the Somerset countryside. Clients are seen on a one-to-one basis, and I am able to teach Reiki and mindfulness to groups from a perfect setting on the beautiful Somerset Levels.

Sometimes I look back on the industry as a whole and wonder what life would be like if I were still running those salons. The buzz excited me, and the industry is ever changing and providing amazing treatments for our twenty-first-century demands: new machines giving superb exfoliating facials, incredible lifting and firming body treatments, and a plethora of nail therapies to confuse even the most proficient therapist, as well as beauty award ceremonies to compete in and a window display to plan for each season. Do I miss it? Sometimes, but if I hadn't had such an amazing time growing and developing the salons, I wouldn't be where I am today. I had always wanted to be self-employed. I had always wanted to own my own salon. I still work for myself to this day, but I work alone, without the stress and strain that often goes alongside the running of a very busy salon.

No one knows what the future holds. When I was at college I wanted to work on the cruise liners. Sadly, in those days two years' salon experience was required before they would even give you an interview. (Today they have their own beauty training centres.) I was 'lucky' on leaving college to be offered the room above the hairdressers. Lucky to have been self-employed from the start of my career, although it was quite daunting, and thankfully my mother had been self-employed for many years, so a trip to her accountant and a loan from my stepfather got me set up with my first couch and a wax pot. I got started. I never did get to see the world on the liners. Not as a therapist, anyway.

There have been so many obstacles in my way. People have come into my life for different reasons and given me help and guidance. I now know why I am here. I know what I must do…and that is to write this book.

CONTENTS

APPARENTLY I AM WRITING A BOOK

I always thought you had to be famous to write a book. A slightly blinkered view, as when I really thought about it, were Deepak Chopra or Eckhart Tolle famous before they wrote their first books? Probably not. I originally didn't think I had a 'market' for it, but as my life has unfolded and I have embraced social media, the feedback I've had from blog posts and tweets is that I really should write. I should write in a way that the average person can understand. I should write as if I am talking to my clients, from a real point of view, of how you can grow and develop without having to sit on a mossy tuffet contemplating your navel.

Timing is everything

This is not aimed as a coffee table self-help book. There are plenty of those on the market; heaven knows my bookshelves are full of them! This is my story. This is the story of a relatively 'normal' girl developing skills that have helped many people in the past and may also help you. I am not a clairvoyant, and I do not have a story of how I used to see spirits as a child with my parents not believing me. I have no scary ghost stories, I do not talk to angels, and I do not see auras. I have developed my intuition over many years in a way that many of you reading this will have. In the course of reading you may begin to realise that you have skills that you never knew you had. You may even have a few 'lightbulb moments' along the way that enable you to see the bigger picture.

As a child, I didn't have any imaginary friends—nor did I see faeries at the bottom of the garden. I was just a normal child of the 1970s in a normal family. My grandmother on my father's side was a churchgoer, and my other grandmother used to say the usual things like, 'You won't go to heaven if…' or 'Nicola, do not blaspheme.' I didn't really understand what she meant, and I didn't take a lot of notice. It was only as I got older that I realised the underlying fear of upsetting 'God' meant you had to be good and that heaven was a place that you went when you died. Or not. Depending on how good you were.

I went to Sunday school for a while but soon got bored, and I'm sure my mother only sent me so she could have a child-free house, enabling her to get some cleaning done. Although I was brought up as Church of England and have been christened, religion was never forced upon me as a child. I attended the usual school carol concerts, and I had carried the banner for the Girl Guides at church in my time. I found it all very boring. Very, very dull and quite depressing. The sermons were all so traumatic and 'deep'. There were never any fun things for the vicar to preach about. Or at least it didn't seem like it, as an early teen. I often wondered why on earth they didn't build churches with windows you could open and let some air through. I didn't understand 'energies' as I understand them now, but I just felt churches were damp, musty, and quite morbid. Why on earth didn't they do this preaching lark outside, like Jesus did?

Interesting, the things you think of as a child. I quite liked the music, though—the Christmas carols and the uplifting pieces, like Handel's *Messiah.* But the dark, depressing hymns didn't interest me at all. Having to gain forgiveness to gain entrance to heaven always seemed like a lot of hard work, when you didn't really need forgiveness in the first place, unless you were really, really bad, and then who gave it to you, anyway? These were questions running around in a child's mind. I was lucky that my parents didn't really push religion upon me, so when in later years I began to work with the subtle energies of the universe, I didn't have a particular belief system to live by. I was able to teach Reiki to all-comers and know that it was not restrictive to any one religion. After all, the universe was here first. It was humankind who decided that they needed to follow a religion. We as humans created a plethora of things to worship.

Now, don't get me wrong. I am not dismissing religion at all. It gives people focus. It gives them hope. But it also causes disharmony and wars: 'My religion is better than yours.' Like children in a playground. Sadly, in this day and age the playground is usually a whole country, and the weapons aren't of the peashooter variety, but nuclear and chemical.

I have friends who are quite 'religious', and I have those who are completely atheist, with many somewhere in between. We all need to believe in something, even if that something is just yourself. This is not a book about religion, and it is not being directly or knowingly channelled, like many other books, but you can't write about the energies of the universe and how we are all now developing so quickly without seeing how religion fits in.

I have treated many people in my time who have deep-rooted 'issues' that can be traced back to believing on a deep level that they are not good enough or deserving enough for God's love, and will therefore die and not go 'somewhere nice'. What a terrible way to live your life. This saddens me greatly, when I see that religion and our upbringings are to blame for this. In my world, there is no right or wrong. Things just *are.* What is right for one person may be wrong for another. None of us should have the right to say to another that it is wrong to *believe* in a particular thing, or in a certain way. Everyone has free will and everyone is different. We must be respectful of one another's beliefs, but when these beliefs begin to create disharmony and fear in the individual, then surely a few things need to be looked at.

Why are we allowing our religious beliefs to affect us so greatly? Why don't we just break free and say NO? Probably because many of you are afraid. You are afraid of what your church or such like will 'do' to you, and ultimately you are afraid that you will not go to heaven when you die.

People are so busy looking outside for answers, plugged into their laptops, tablets, and phones, that they have lost the ability to really see the essence of the human race. They are too absorbed in the 'what ifs' instead of just taking a moment to just be. To just be and experience and enjoy. To be fully absorbed in your life.

We forget that we are spiritual beings in human bodies, and that we are here to experience life. We are so wound up with everything that we miss it, and before we know it, it is too late. It's gone.

So wake up and smell the coffee…or the roses!

This book is aimed at those who feel that something is missing in their lives. Those who sometimes, or all the time, feel that they are treading in treacle or taking three steps forward and two steps back. I will attempt to talk to you as a real human to another human, and not as some scientific professor or angelic channel from the ether. I have many clients who would like to free themselves of the constraints and stresses of everyday life, but they find the books they have read, or the talks they have been to, far too confusing. They like the way I speak, and they need a little book to refer to. Some people reading this may find it too simple; some may find it just right. After all, just as we have to find the therapies that work for us or the hairdresser that just 'gets us', we also need to find the perfect book or the teacher.

How many times have you bought a book on a friend's recommendation and just not 'got it'? I was introduced to *Conversations with God,* by Neal Donald Walsh, back in 2002, and it took me four years to actually take it off the shelf in my office and read it. So, if this book doesn't make sense, or you feel you have heard it all before, pop it on a shelf and come back to it. Or pass it on to someone else who may benefit. Some books come into our paths and are life changing, but if you come back to them years later, you find them boring or worthless. Just remember that at the time it was a very worthwhile read. You no longer need it, but many books are catalysts to greater things.

When I was a child, I bought a book on how to read auras from W. H. Smith, many years before the Internet, and years before Waterstones was on the high street. Self-help, esoteric, spiritual sections in bookshops were just not there. You either had sections for the Bible or those with a few newfangled diet books—like *The Pineapple Diet*! (I'm showing my age now!) I'm not sure which section I found this little gem in, but I was drawn to it. I was a little embarrassed about purchasing something so off-piste, and I didn't dare tell my parents. I am sure they would have thought I had gone a little weird. But that was just my assumption, and assumptions are worthless and a waste of energy. I know this now!

To say I really understood the book would be lying. I read it and desperately wanted to be able to 'see' these wonderful colours around people. It never happened. I got frustrated after trying so hard. The book went on a shelf and I forgot about it until many years later, when I started working with Reiki and found many people in my path that could see auras—but I still couldn't.

It took many more years in my own development to actually realise that every person is different. We all have gifts and we all have different abilities. I spent a great deal of time wanting so badly to 'see' angels, auras, and signs. I wanted to hear the voices and have a guide to help me along my pathway, just as my friends did.

A few years ago, a good friend visited me. She channels angels and paints stunning works of art by connecting with the angelic realms. She is very intuitive, psychic, and one of

those people who would stop in the middle of a conversation and say, 'Hold on, *they* are telling me something.' She gave me some quite profound advice: 'Nicki, you *really* don't want to hear angels in your head. It can be so annoying. They really do get in the way sometimes. Use your own gifts.'

What gifts? Help me, please! 'You are clairsentient. You feel. You are intuitive. You don't need to *see* spirits, angels, or guides. You don't need proof. That's all you are looking for. Proof. You can do it. Whatever you think 'it' is. You are you, and you do what *you* do. Stop trying so hard to see in a visual way. You already know.'

That was a big lightbulb moment. Yes, there are books to help you attune, relax, meditate, and connect. There are people out there to help you along your way, and to help you as a human being connect with your spirit and higher self. There are so many ways to realise that we are all connected. There are science-based books, spiritual-based books, and hopefully books like this. I am not a scientist. I certainly don't have a degree in quantum physics, nor have I climbed mountains and physically walked in the path of the Shaman. I have not spent months in a monastery on silent retreats or given away all my worldly goods to release me of any sin. I have just developed myself over my years on this planet. We are all here to learn something and to develop in some way. Some books I read and I just don't understand, because I find them too deep. Other books and people I am drawn to and learn from, just like finding a good hairdresser that suits you. There are many out there. Some come and go, and some stay for many years. Find your own path. There is a great little saying:

Just because your friends aren't on the same path as you,

Doesn't mean they have gotten lost.

I am just me: a normal person finding my way and now being able to help other quite normal people realise that they also don't need to do anything out of their comfort zones to connect with their inner spirits and realise their dreams.

People come into your life for a reason, a season, or a lifetime.

Reason, Season, or Lifetime

People come into your life for a reason, a season, or a lifetime.

When you figure out which one it is,

you will know what to do for each person.

When someone is in your life for a REASON,

it is usually to meet a need you have expressed.

They have come to assist you through a difficulty;

to provide you with guidance and support;

to aid you physically, emotionally, or spiritually.

They may seem like a godsend, and they are.

They are there for the reason you need them to be.

Then, without any wrongdoing on your part or at an inconvenient time,

this person will say or do something to bring the relationship to an end.

Sometimes they die. Sometimes they walk away.

Sometimes they act up and force you to take a stand.

What we must realize is that our need has been met, our desire fulfilled; their work is done.

The prayer you sent up has been answered, and now it is time to move on.

Some people come into your life for a SEASON,

because your turn has come to share, grow, or learn.

They bring you an experience of peace or make you laugh.

They may teach you something you have never done.

They usually give you an unbelievable amount of joy.

Believe it. It is real. But only for a season.

LIFETIME relationships teach you lifetime lessons,

things you must build upon in order to have a solid emotional foundation.

Your job is to accept the lesson, love the person,

and put what you have learned to use in all other relationships and areas of your life.

It is said that love is blind but friendship is clairvoyant.

—*Unknown*

LIGHTBULB MOMENTS

There have been many of these throughout my life, although some of them were not actually noticed at the time—more of an aftereffect, an 'aha!' when someone pointed something out that really made sense. Sometimes things just click and my first big experience of this was when I realised that I no longer wanted to own my two salons. I wanted to change the life plan.

The saying 'A plan is a basis for change' has always been thrown around our household, as dates alter and times are never set in stone: always write in pencil, never in pen. I always liked to run my life in an ordered way, and when I married into a military lifestyle, I had to bend a little. I had to use that pencil a little more often, and then one day I really had a lightbulb moment. I myself decided to implement the rule-changing process. The life plan that I had made completely shifted. I had built up two salons. I had staff and I had responsibilities. I was making plans and manifesting my dreams. My dream was to have four salons by the time I was forty, brand them, and sell them all as a chain. I had the blueprint, and it was working. I had avidly watched the DVD of *The Secret,* by Rhonda Byrne, well before it was available in the UK. Since then it has become a household name in the manifesting world for beginners, and it is also a book. Some find it too simple; some find it life changing. It's a great starting point.

As my businesses evolved over the years and the salons grew, the beauty industry changed, and so did employment laws. Business rates kept increasing, and VAT took a leap from 15 percent to 17.5

percent. Everything was becoming more difficult rather than easier. I found I was working all the hours in the day and most of the evenings, and Sundays were spent doing paperwork. I wasn't quite big enough to employ a bookkeeper, and I still enjoyed the practical side of treating people. I had been to the seminars and read all the books: really successful business people worked 'on' their businesses and not in them, but I wasn't prepared to stop treating people just yet. I was holding on.

In 2005 I had the privilege of receiving a treatment from a superb holistic therapist, Ben Barnett, who used to hire space in my salons to do hydrotherm treatments for my clients. He was the area trainer for this beautiful massage system, which involves the client lying face up on top of warm, water-filled pillows. Totally supported by the water, there is no need to turn over halfway through the treatment, so there is total relaxation right from the start. Often with massage, a client will not 'give up' and relax until halfway through, as subliminally they know at some point that the turning-over process will have to be done.

Ben had started to develop this treatment further with a guided meditation technique that enabled the client to reach a deeper state of relaxation. Often people hold tension in areas of their bodies even the deepest massage cannot physically iron out. As we have learnt more and more about the connection between physical tension and emotional issues, some holistic therapists have begun to work at the root of the problem, which is usually emotion-based, and when that issue is addressed it in turn releases tensions within the body. This is a vast subject, and there are many detailed books that highlight this. The first one I read was *You Can Heal Your Life*, by Louisa L. Hay (1984).

As Ben was developing this superb therapy, he used me as a guinea pig. I was not as developed spiritually or energetically in those days, and sometimes I found Ben quite difficult to understand. Having said that, I found him fascinating and just wanted to learn everything all at once. I used to become very frustrated that he was such a powerful healer, and I desperately wanted to be able to treat the way he did. Remember what I said earlier in the book about everyone having different gifts? Well, Ben has a unique connection with the universe. A way of bringing voice-directed meditation and visualisation together with massage to enable the client to create wonderful things.

Remember...

People take different roads seeking fulfilment and happiness.

Just because they're not on your road doesn't meant they've gotten lost.

—Dalai Lama

Ben's treatments are not for everyone. Not everyone is 'ready', and not everyone will understand the process although I am sure Ben would say that it is not meant to be understood, but to be experienced. Our over thinking brains try to analyse everything. We try to put everything into boxes and process it, rather than going with the flow and accepting. My treatment with Ben was a lightbulb moment, a very powerful turning point in my life, and for this I will be ever grateful.

He asked what I wanted to create from the treatment—one thing. I wanted two. Obviously I would want two; I wanted my money's worth. I wanted to be proud and peaceful, as I had realised over the years that I wasn't feeling any pride in what I had achieved. I was feeling stressed and resentful. I was running around like a hamster in a wheel, and I am sure if I knew then what I know now about mindfulness, I would have never been in that position. I would probably have the four salons, but then I wouldn't have had this 'journey', and I wouldn't be writing this book.

Everything happens for a reason.

It happens for a reason even though sometimes, when your life changes and shifts, it throws you off course and leaves you with no idea of the bigger picture. That's where trust comes in.

The finer details of my treatment are quite a blur. I just remember an image about lifting yourself above your business and seeing it in a glass box, so you can view it from above. I also remember my hands were gripping the couch so hard I couldn't let go. I was unable to let go of all that I had worked for. The outcome, after a huge 'shift' and many tears, was that I didn't want to do this anymore. I wanted out. Out of the business, not the treatment—there was no way I was getting out of that!

Plans are a basis for change.

This was a catalyst and a lightbulb moment.

A very BIG lightbulb!

The rest, they say, is history, but there was quite a process involved. I certainly didn't dress and walk downstairs, telling my staff I wanted to sell up. It was a finely tuned process. It was a whole year of planning before we even told them. The process was then in full swing, but there were a few more lightbulb moments along the way. During that time, I caught myself saying to new clients as they looked around the salons, 'Oh yes, I am very proud of it.'

Pow! I actually felt a warm, glowing feeling of pride, rather than resentment over all the never-ending hard work. I was proud, and I could then use this energy to help sell the sa-

lons. Without this, it would have been a very hard process. People want to know why you are 'giving up'. I wasn't giving up. I was moving on. The question was what did I want to do for the next fifteen years? Work 'on' the business and stop treating people, or sell up, go smaller, and specialise in what I do now? Until I began to see that plans really are a basis for change, I couldn't move on. I had choices to make. I could choose to stay and grow even bigger,

I *could* do it, I chose not to. I chose to move on. I had been there, done that, as they say.

Oh, and the peacefulness I'd asked Ben for? Well, I became a great deal more peaceful after making the decision and stating my intention. I took longer walks with my dog. I spent more time in mindful moments, before the wave of mindfulness workshops and training ever became popular.

I love a good lightbulb moment. It's just a shame that many people don't notice them.

Watch out! They sometimes catch you unawares.

JOURNEYS, PATHWAYS, AND CROSSROADS.

That overused word 'journey' makes me cringe—overused by those on reality television, often in a competition for singing, dancing, or ice-skating. It used to be a word used by those seeking spiritual enlightenment, but now everyone uses it, often without thinking about exactly what it means to them. We are all here to experience life. We are all on a 'journey'. We all have pathways to choose, and we all have choices to make. It is part of being human, and we are beginning to realise this. As a human race, we are beginning to wake up and realise that life is for living, and there really is a purpose to it all. We are gradually getting off the hamster wheel of monotony and seeing the bigger picture.

People are realising that, in the grand scheme of things, life is short. We are making 'bucket lists', and with the development of the Internet in the last twenty years, it is much easier to plan holidays where lifelong desires can be realised. We are climbing mountains, travelling to the depths of the rain forests, and helping with conservation in remote areas of the world. People feel they need to try skydiving, white-water rafting, jungle trekking, and scuba diving. Some choose to do charity work. Others enroll in college courses and take qualifications they never had a chance to when they were young.

Sometimes a life can seem quite uneventful—no extreme sports and no international holidays—but everyone has a life in front of them. What feels right for one may not interest another. This is what makes us all different and so unique.

There used to be a delightful shop in Taunton, just a short walk from my salon. It sold incense, books, Indian feathers and dream catchers, crystals, and angel cards. It was called Pathways and was owned by the most wonderful woman, called Bev. One of those people you feel you already know. I used to pop in and out, sometimes purchasing, sometimes just absorbing the atmosphere. Then it closed, which was such a shame, as it was the only shop of its kind in the town, and the nearest alternative was a forty-minute drive to Glastonbury.

I bumped into Bev while walking my dog a few months after she had closed. She had her own plan and her own pathway to follow. The closing of the shop was something she had needed to do. We chatted, we parted, and then I would spot her again in the town every few months—those chance meetings along a pavement, where you nod, say hello, and hurry along. Now, in the six years since I have moved from my salon in the centre of town, I must have bumped into Bev about half a dozen times. For a while, each time we saw each other there were a few words, a smile, and a warm exchange of energies. Then I noticed a request had come through on my website from someone called 'Pathways' to be added to the newsletter list. It had to be Bev! There had always been some kind of unspoken energetic connection between us. Pathways are funny things; they send you in all sorts of directions—sometimes the direct motorway route, sometimes the more picturesque scenic route, and sometimes a mountainous hike!

Then, very recently, I popped to town later than usual on my day off. One coffee later, I was on my way out of the restaurant when I bumped headlong into Bev. She hadn't been in there before and was checking it out for a possible ladies lunch. *Synchronicity.*

'Time for a coffee?' I asked.

'Why not?' She grinned, and we made our way to the closest table.

Ninety minutes later we had caught up and swapped information, and I had the confirmation I needed about my book writing. Chance meetings over the years may well have seemed like little nods of hello across a shop floor or a pavement, but there had been much

more to it than that. During our little catch-up, I was able to coax Bev onto Twitter, by showing her how it had enabled me to build an even wider client base from all over the country, and she gave me the confidence to start writing. This, in my world, is called synchronicity. Some call it a coincidence, but really there is no such thing. Everything happens for a reason, even if that reason is not apparent at the time. Our pathways had crossed many times over the years without either of us realising the bigger picture or the reason, and I am sure that our paths will cross again in the future.

We are all on a pathway or a journey. We are experiencing things all the time. All of us have a story to tell, and the older we become the more wisdom we have, the more roads we have travelled, and the more stories we have—and, with any luck, more answers.

The crossroads? Well, we have all had those. A road trip wouldn't be much fun without a few crossroads to negotiate. No doubt there will also be a few chicanes along the way and some very uneven, bumpy lanes, but effectively, we all end up in the same place. We just have different ways of getting there. The key is seeing a crossroads as a collection of choices. Looking back on your life, I am sure you will be able to remember many times when you have said, 'I should have never done that', or, 'If only I hadn't taken that job/car/house.' Well, you did. You made a choice at that time. You may have been given a few options, and you chose one.

Was it the 'right one'? Well, remember, there is no such thing as right or wrong. Things just *are.* A plan is a basis for change; it isn't set in stone. If you don't like the pathway you are on, you can change direction. You can't go back, but you can find an alternative route. That route may well be up a mountain or down a slippery slope, but it's workable, and it's a choice you are free to make. You can even get off a motorway if you wait for the next slip road.

Many years ago my husband, at the age of nearly forty, was reaching his 'break point' in the Royal Navy, where he had been an aircrewman on Sea King helicopters for twenty years. There had once been an option to offer people an additional ten-year contract, after they served twenty, but this was stopped due to his job being taken over by the Royal Marines, and he was faced with a choice: stay and hope that he *may* be offered an extension, or accept an offer of a job within the RAF for the next ten years. This wasn't an easy switchover; it meant leaving the Royal Navy, a service he had joined as a young man straight out of school, and one he loved. It also meant joining what he had always regarded as 'the enemy', with all the upheaval that entailed, and later on a move to work in Northern Ireland for a few years. This was workable, but a big choice to make. We made the decision together. He moved over and had the immense pleasure of working on the old soon-to-be-retired Wessex helicopters in Ireland, something he had always wanted to do. Afterwards, he was offered a much sought-after instructional role in a brand-new squadron, flying the new Merlin helicopter at RAF Benson.

There were good things and bad things about the move. Most were subjective, depending on the way you looked at it, and it would be inappropriate to list all the pros and cons here, but suffice to say, there were many times when I heard him say, 'I should never have joined the RAF.' Many, many times.

Since my evolution in the more esoteric ways of the universe and my understanding of right and wrong, I was able to 'check' him when he said, 'I should never have done that.' I was able to say, 'But you did. We made the choice together, and at the time it was the right thing to do. If it no longer serves you, change it, but don't beat yourself up about it.'

However, regrets and resentment can get in the way of so many things in your life path. Many people spend their lives with regrets—the 'if only' and the 'I shouldn't have'. Sometimes these remarks may just be flippant and offhand, but more often, as words are powerful, they leave an imprint. They make you really believe you have spoken the truth. This 'I shouldn't have' way of thinking uses unnecessary energy. Anything you put your attention on will grow. You will end up spending your whole life regretting things and have resentment over the event and possibly towards the people directly involved with your choice.

But it's only a choice. All you did was take a path, start a journey, and realise you didn't like it. When you take responsibility for your choice, and see it as just that, a choice, you can move along. Like a board game: move on.

I'm not one for taking all the skeletons out of the cupboard and letting them run around scaring you half to death. Nor am I one for shutting everything away, never to be seen or heard of again. There has to be some balance along the way. Everything you have done is part of your story. Like a movie, it defines you. Everything you have done, in your eyes good or bad, has been done. It's happened. It is a defining point in your life, never to be seen again. Acceptance is essential. Take responsibility for what you chose to do, and choose what to do now.

The only thing you can be certain of is the moment that is NOW! Pow! And that moment has now gone. This brings us nicely to the next chapter, on being mindful.

PRESENT-MOMENT AWARENESS.

We take care of the future best by taking care of the present now.

—Jon Kabat-Zinn

Modern life is, for many, increasingly stressful. We are all subjected to pressures from many different sources. Work becomes ever busier, with many working longer and longer hours. Relationships are juggled; family life gets stretched between everyday worries and our need to be 'on the go' all the time. This modern way of living can cause problems with our health and well-being. It was the continuing stress of running two large salons that made me realise I needed a change of path. Maybe if I had come across these techniques then, my path would have been different. On reflection, though, I wouldn't be here writing this book for you. As my stress levels increased and my demeanour became more manic and busy, I knew that I had to do something about it. If I had chosen to stay, then that would be a different story, but I decided to leave before my lifestyle made me ill.

Many illnesses are now proven to be stress related. Not just the visible panic attacks and anxiety, but also high blood pressure, increased cholesterol, and digestive issues such as IBS and heartburn. Depression and anxiety, stress, and lack of confidence are all on a sliding scale. With some people these symptoms ebb and flow, being part of your life and part of your story. For others a lifetime of suffering from depression can be quite debilitating, and medication is sometimes needed. Some are able to find a variety of therapies to help them cope, while others feel exhausted with all the trying to find solutions and feeling powerless to change things—often caught in the 'poor me' syndrome, with too much time spent wishing they were somewhere or someone else. Too much energy is often given to ruminating over unwanted thoughts.

Mindfulness enhances our awareness of moment-to-moment experience in everyday life.

By focusing on what is happening in the present moment and developing kind, nonjudgmental attitudes towards ourselves, we can learn to develop a different relationship with what upsets the balance and causes disharmony within the body and mind. We can become deeply attuned to our breath and our bodies, learning to be aware of thoughts and emotions. The key here is to become *aware* of and not overwhelmed by our mind chatter. We can become better able to manage limiting thoughts and emotions, and we can discover new ways of responding intelligently to difficulties, rather than reacting in old, often unhelpful automatic patterns.

The mindfulness approach was developed by Jon Kabat-Zinn in the late 1970s. It draws from ancient Eastern philosophies, but back in those days it was seen as quite secular in its approach, with people thinking they had to be part of a religious movement in order to meditate. The more modern way of teaching 'mindfulness-based stress reduction' (MBSR) has been designed to suit the more modern world.

Mindfulness has recently become a real buzzword, and I hope people won't think it is a phase or a trend. It is the most perfect way to keep our bodies and minds healthy without having to spend hours on end gazing at our navels! Research over three decades supports this relatively new approach to enabling people to cope more effectively with their everyday stress and anxiety, and of helping to increase feelings of well-being while decreasing the impact modern-day living has on health. Practicing mindfulness has been shown to decrease pain, increase immunity, and lower blood pressure, with conditions such as IBS, fibromyalgia, and chronic fatigue being helped considerably. Recovery from operations, illness, and cancer therapies can all be speeded up with mindfulness.

Your life can become enhanced considerably when you practice mindfulness, and this does not involve sitting on a mossy tuffet! There are many books on the subject, but some are an easier read than others. I particularly like *Mindfulness for Busy People*, by Dr Michael Sinclair and Dr Josie Seydel. If you really don't want to purchase another book, then read on. Although I didn't intend this book to be 'another coffee table self-help book', many people have asked for a few sections with some practical help as well as showing how these techniques have helped me personally. So onwards we go!

Take a Moment in Your Day

This is a short exercise that should take fifteen to twenty minutes. With practice it can be done much more quickly and will become part of your everyday life, enabling you to 'check in' with how your body feels within just a few moments. So many of us rush about from day to day, not actually feeling how our bodies are responding to various emotions and stimuli until the stress builds to such a degree that illness occurs and we just have to stop. If you have never done this before, it may take a few attempts to actually see the benefits, so don't give up. It may be something you already practice, or that you haven't done for a while. Take what you need from this section, and skip it completely if you are already a mindfulness convert!

A restless body can be a sign of a restless mind.

Sit or lie down. Be comfortable. Place a pillow under your knees if you are lying down. Keep your feet on the floor if seated. Take your shoes off. Feel the ground beneath your feet. Have a blanket over you if necessary, so you are warm but not overheated.

You may need someone to calmly and slowly read the guided checklist to you. Read it yourself first, and see how you feel. This is why mindfulness courses and workshops are often superb for beginners, so they can be talked through the process, allowing them to focus on their bodies.

- 'Check in' with your body just as it is right now. Notice the sensations that are present, feeling the contact the body is making with the floor or chair. Take a moment to notice.
- Begin to scan the body. Take your awareness through different parts, without judging what you are aware of, but as best you can bring attention to your experience moment to moment.
- Start with the top of the head. Notice sensations. Feel the weight of the head as it rests on the floor or cushion, and become aware of the forehead, noticing whether or not you can feel the pulse, whether there is tightness or ease. Move to the eyes, the nose, cheeks, mouth, and chin, and finally to the ears, including any sounds that you notice coming to

the ears. Become aware moment by moment of the changing pattern of sensations, feelings of warmth, and ease. Notice how your head feels on your shoulders if you are seated.

- Letting go of the head and face, move your attention and awareness to the neck and shoulders, noticing the strong muscles in this part of the body, having awareness of any tension in the neck and throat, perhaps becoming aware of the sensation of air in the throat—something you wouldn't normally do.
- Now to the shoulders. Feel the contact your shoulder blades have with the floor. Stretch your attention into the arms, elbows, wrists, hands, and every finger. Be aware of any sensations in each moment.
- Move your focus to the chest area, noticing the subtle rise and fall of the chest with the in-and-out breath, turning your awareness to the ribcage, the front and back and sides

of the ribs, the upper back resting on the floor. Notice any aches and pains here, and see if you can bring a sense of gentleness and kindness to these areas.

- Turn your awareness now to the abdomen and stomach, the place where we have our 'gut feelings'. Notice your attitude towards this part of your body. See if you can allow it to be as it is, taking a relaxed and accepting approach to this part of the body. Move your awareness to the lower back, the lumbar spine, feeling the gentle pressure as the back meets the floor before moving your awareness to the pelvis area, the hip bones, the sitting bones, and the groin, noticing any sensations or lack of sensations that are here, perhaps being aware of the breath in this part of the body. If you are seated, feel your 'seat bones' on the chair. Notice if you are sitting evenly.
- Let go of the torso. As your awareness moves on through the body, take your attention into the thighs of both legs,

feeling the weight of the legs, gently noticing what other sensations there are here. Tune into the skin, bone, and muscle of the legs.

- Turn your attention gently towards the knees. Notice if there is any discomfort here, and if there is none, then notice anything else, such as the feel of your knees against your clothes or the blanket.
- Stretch into the calves and notice how your muscles feel, checking where your attention is from time to time and noticing the quality of your attention, seeing if it is possible to bring a gentleness and kindness into your awareness. Try not to force yourself. Just bring lightness to your attention in this part of the body.
- Finally, pay attention to your feet—the heels, the instep, and the balls of the feet, the tops of the feet, skin and bone, and finally the toes—seeing if it is possible to distinguish one

toe from another. Notice whether there is tension here—sensations, numbness, tingling—and allow any tension to soften as you bring gentle attention to it. Be aware.

- Now take one or two deeper breaths and widen your focus, filling the whole body with awareness, noticing whatever is present, sweeping the body with your awareness from top to bottom.
- Experience the body from the inside out. Notice whether there is any non acceptance towards any parts of the body as you fill the body with a gentle awareness. See if you can have compassion for any judgments or for any tensions or pain that might be present as you notice them. Feel the energy of life flowing through you.

Rest in awareness of your amazing body.

Have compassion for its pains and appreciation for its capabilities and its sheer wonder.

During this process you may notice that your mind is wandering, and this is perfectly natural. It's what minds do. Just be *aware* that your mind has wandered, and gently guide it back to the part of the body you are focusing on. It is so easy to become frustrated in yourself when your mind wanders off, but this is not a Zen-type meditation, it is an awareness exercise, so don't beat yourself up about what you think you should be doing. Just go with it.

There are many different exercises you can do, and some lovely guided mediation downloads and CDs to purchase. Finding one that suits you can be a tricky process. I personally don't like guided CDs, but many students do. You must find your own way.

Breath Work

What is this weirdness that people call 'breath work'? It's actually a softer way to introduce people to meditation; and 'meditation' is a word that scares many people. The word often conjures up images of yogis sitting cross-legged at the top of a mountain, but it honestly doesn't have to be like that. We are living in a modern world. We have busy lives. Stress and stress-related illness are seen more and more, manifesting in different ways. We are all human. Knowing what to do to relieve these stresses is what matters.

Let's start here...

Take a moment. Sit or lie down. Be comfortable. Place a pillow under your knees if you are lying down. Keep your feet on the floor if seated. Take your shoes off. Feel the ground beneath your feet. You must take time to make yourself comfortable.

Now close your eyes. Don't 'do' anything. Just settle. Just *be.*

Focus on your breathing. Don't 'do' anything with it. Just watch it. Take a moment.

Watch your breath.

Then count. Count how long it takes you to breathe in…Don't try to change the length.

Just *be* aware.

Count in…count out.

After about six breaths, you will notice you naturally slow down.

Now extend the count by one second.

Everyone will breathe a different length of breath. Everyone is different. Your natural breath pattern may be a count of seven or eight. It could be longer.

As you count and extend, you will be focusing—focusing just on your breath. Nothing else. That is meditating. Focusing on one thing.

Your body will become heavier. Your breathing will deepen. Start there.

If thoughts of 'What shall I have for supper?' pop into your mind, then watch the thoughts pass by. Try not to engage in the conversation of 'Shall I pop to the shops? Where is my list? What time is it?'

Just allow the thought to pass by - like a cloud.

And refocus.

On your breath.

When you are ready, take a few deep breaths and have a stretch. Bring your awareness back to where you are.

Just five minutes a day can make all the difference. When you understand the concept, you can do this on a train, at your desk, or in the park. Then you can develop even further. But start here.

Start with the *breath.*

When you have understood this quite simple but powerful concept, you will find that taking five minutes in your day to do this simple exercise will really help your stress levels.

Practice * Breathe * Meditate * Simple

You have probably all heard the beautiful song by Simon and Garfunkel, “The Sound of Silence.”

Is there such a thing? Does silence have a sound? Or is it a bit like the saying, ‘If a tree falls in the forest and there is no one to hear it, does it make a sound?’ There is always sound, if you really listen. When you are peaceful, mindful, and just be-ing, there is always a sound. If you listen, even if you are in a soundproof room, you will always be able to hear your breath. Your breath is sound. The sound of your body.

The most amazing focal point of all that is, is your breath.

Respect your breath.

You are the breath.

I realised this most profoundly when I was having a float—another defining moment in my life, when I found out exactly what being in a flotation tank was all about. The only thing you can hear is your breath, and it is an amazing feeling. The perfect space to really 'hear' your body. Flotation tanks have come a long way in the past ten years and the one I visited was almost as big as a whole room. Thinking it was going to be claustrophobic and boring, I was soon to be pleasantly surprised. The aim was to have the float after a powerful unraveling massage where the weightlessness created by floating could allow your muscles to relax and your body to realign. This perfect combination of therapies is something I highly recommend. During the time spent floating, your breath becomes a very powerful tool for relaxation and focus.

Some of you may need some coaching to be able to master the above little exercise; others will be reading this and thinking it's all old hat. Take from this what you like. There are many more exercises that can help to reduce stress and increase your mindfulness. One very powerful exercise is mindful eating.

Mindful Eating

Eating is one of those daily activities that we usually do on automatic pilot. When we become more mindful, we become aware of our reasons for eating as we do: Why are we craving that biscuit? Why are we staring in the fridge? We have inbuilt belief systems regarding food, including rules and expectations. We have preconceived ideas about greed or wastefulness. When we bring mindfulness to the dinner table, it is a useful way to tap into the calming effects of the present moment. When we eat with mindfulness, we bring awareness to all of the aspects of the experience.

In the workshops I now run, I talk the participants through a great little exercise using a raisin. Although this technique can be found in many books and online, I find people respond better if they can be talked through the process, and for that reason I have chosen not to include it in this book. Instead I ask that you take some *time* to actually experience your food. Do you like what you see, smell, and taste? Do you appreciate where the food came from? Are you grateful for the food you are eating? An attitude of gratitude can make you feel quite different. I believe that eating mindfully gives you a deeper way of connecting with the pleasurable way of nourishing yourself through food, as opposed to ploughing through a plate of food to satisfy a hunger.

More often than not, the food that you really take time over is the food in that lovely restaurant that you have taken time to choose. This is often the only time when you take a moment to absorb the presentation of the food on the plate, to use your senses to smell, and to decide where to start eating! You even take time to cut the first morsel. You are being mindful. In reality, on a day-to-day basis, this never occurs when you are eating your sandwich at work, still sat at your desk while swilling a coffee and answering the phone. It only takes a moment to 'down tools' and savour that sandwich. Your digestive tract will thank you for that little extra saliva being used as you chew a little slower and help the digestive process get underway, rather than hardly chewing your food at all.

Food is about nourishment of the body, not just filling the gap of hunger. Many people teach mindful eating as simply 'eating slowly, without distraction'. This works; it gives you time to enjoy your food. But I believe that mindful eating encompasses the entire process of eating.

Begin to gain awareness of your body and the cues and the triggers for eating. Are you really hungry? Or do you just like the idea of the food that you see? This doesn't mean that you shouldn't be able to walk past a shop selling delicious cakes and not be drawn in to purchase one. I am just saying that you should be aware of what draws you in. Be present and be aware. Be *mindful.*

Some foods you will eat for nourishment, some for pure enjoyment—think Easter eggs! You don't actually get any real nourishment at all from one, but you enjoy it. Notice that. You don't need to feel guilty about eating it; just appreciate it with mindfulness. Think about when you are on holiday in a warm foreign country: you often take more time to enjoy and savour your food as you experience new flavours and textures for the first time. The weather is usually warmer, so you eat more salads and need less fuel. Be aware of your reasons for eating.

This broad application of your reason for eating makes mindful eating a powerful tool for developing a healthier, happier relationship with food. If you are a healthy eater and make fresh juices, take your time drinking them. Be aware. This is not about dieting and losing weight. This exercise is about being aware of your body: being in the moment and becoming respectful of your food and the nourishment it gives you.

There are many little exercises out there for you to try, and I appreciate that many of you have families, with mealtimes being a little fraught. If you have very young children, try to feed them first so they can be settled while you take time for yourself to enjoy your meal mindfully. As your children grow up, teach them to respect their food as well. Teach them where the foods on their plate come from and make mealtimes a space for taking time. No bolting down food in order to get out of the door to see friends or to get back to watching the television. Children have developing taste buds, and this is an ideal time in their lives to get them to experience different tastes and textures. Just because you don't like something doesn't mean they will dislike it too, but they will take their cue from you. Let them experience for themselves.

To sum up...

The previous breath work and the body scan exercises will help to bring you to the here and now. Practiced daily, it will become a quicker process and will enhance your health and well-being.

When you begin to focus on something we do every day like eating, your mindful experience will unfold even more.

Mindfulness is not, however, a way of blocking out all the 'stuff' that is causing your stress. Some people think they can just close their eyes, 'Ohmmm', and everything will be better. In an ideal world, yes, you could, but what is an ideal world? Aren't we meant to be here to *experience* things? Realising how situations affect you is the first step. Then you can move on. You are not ignoring it, nor becoming aloof and unapproachable—you are becoming aware.

Thoughts are not facts, but they can cause disharmony and disease within the body.

Mindfulness gives you focus.

Becoming mindful offers you a way of staying present and gives you another place from which to view things. You can begin to live life from another perspective—a more colourful, less fragmented, more complete place in which to deal with any stress life deals to you. Mindfulness gives you a sense of peace. Your life is full of experiences, and it is how you deal with what life gives you that really matters. Becoming more mindful makes us more aware of our thoughts and helps free us of habitual methods of reacting. Mindfulness helps us respond with more skill. Using our breath, we can focus. We can notice our feelings, notice how situations make us feel, rather than over thinking them. As I say to many of my students, I can't take away all the rubbish stuff in your life, but I can help you realise how to deal with it without getting so stressed!

When your day starts to go pear shaped, the trick is to take a moment and breathe. Notice how your body is feeling. Notice your breath quickening, your shoulders hunching, your face starting to frown, or your jaw beginning to clench. STOP. Take a breath. In fact, make it at least three slow, controlled, counted breaths. This will enable you to focus only on that. Then notice, how do you feel? How does the situation make your body feel? How is this situation making you feel and react? Now change your reaction into response.

Sit in the present moment. How would you like to respond?

There is no such thing as good or bad. Things just are. What is good for one may be bad for another. You can decide what to do in any situation by switching your thoughts. Firstly acknowledge the thought or emotion without trying to change it. This does not mean you have to like it. You just take it. Acknowledge it and accept it as it is. Be mindful of it. This takes time, and it is a process that you may need to work on. The key is to notice.

Then state something like, 'This makes me feel angry', or, 'This makes me feel sad.' Stating something brings it into perspective. After you identify the issue in the moment, the change in your perception will be easier. Redirect your full attention to your breath. Allow your attention to expand into the whole of your body, along with your breath. Bring kindness into your being. When you 'take a moment', the unnecessary thoughts will move aside and you will be able to focus on the more pressing issues, enabling you to respond from a better perspective. The 'issue' will still be there, but your perception will have changed.

Our ability to think differentiates our species from all others and is miraculous beyond compare. But if we are not careful, our thinking can crowd out other equally precious and miraculous facets of our being. Wakefulness is often the first casualty. Awareness is not the same as thought. It lies beyond thinking, although it makes use of thinking, honouring its value and its power. Awareness is more like a vessel which can hold and contain our thinking, helping us to see and know our thoughts as thoughts rather than getting caught up in theme as reality.

—Jon Kabat-Zinn, from *Mindfulness Meditation for Everyday Life*

MANIFESTING MADE EASY

This is such a huge subject! There are many books you can read and seminars that you can attend, and so many life coaches and inspirational mentors to follow. It wasn't until recently, during a Twitter conversation with the journalist Louise Hulland, that I realised there was a need for a manifesting manual written in a more down-to-earth way, by a grounded person. So many people get confused with the esoteric way of creating and manifesting and can spend a lot of time and energy reading books that don't actually make sense to them. People who had been reading my blog posts and tweets about this subject wanted more information.

Manifesting is a way to attract things and conditions into our lives involving a more direct use of the mind and psychic forces. The use of manifesting increases what is perceived as 'luck'. In the real world there is no such thing as luck, just as there is no such thing as good or bad—things just are. When you understand manifesting, people and resources become more available to help you achieve your goals. Ideas come more easily, and there is usually a higher level of motivation to do what you need to do. However, it is not all about cosmic ordering, as if the universe were one big mail-order catalogue. It's about aligning you with the right flow of energy and *feeling* it.

Your thoughts are actually the cause of most of the events in your life. If you think something, you will be attracting it. Thoughts cause things to happen, and your feelings and emotions are the effect of your thoughts. Thoughts create emotion and emotions can consume you, whether good, bad, happy, or sad. Emotions make us human. If you are thinking 'bad' thoughts, you will feel bad. Look back at the mindfulness exercises in chapter four and take a breath. Then, Take a few deeper breaths and ask yourself how you are feeling right now, in this moment. Take a moment and notice.

Before you can even begin to manifest things in your life, you need to be able to stop, take a moment, and focus on where you are right now. Then it's time to switch your thoughts. When you become aware, you will notice more 'coincidences' happening along your path. Notice how sometimes when you think of someone, he calls, or you spot him or her in the street? I like to call this synchronicity, although many will call it coincidence. In my world there is no such thing as a coincidence. We are all connected by threads of amazing energy. Some of us are more aware of this than others, and the more you quieten your mind and direct your awareness within, the more you will begin to align yourself with the beautiful divine energy that connects you to the world beyond—the world that is beyond time and space as we know it.

Mindfulness exercises and meditation can help greatly with this process. It's all about becoming aware of what we really are. We are all energy. If you like the more scientific aspect of things, you may want to look into the subject of quantum physics. As I said in the introduction, I am not a physicist and find some of the 'deeper' books quite difficult to understand, but I am thankful that scientists finally have actual facts that show we are all vibrating particles of energy, and that we are all in some way or another connected to each other. Many spiritual teachers have been saying this for centuries, but as 'thinking' beings, we now require actual proof. As a race, we have begun to lose our 'feelings' and are needing something more—proof!

Thank heavens for the scientists! Einstein discovered that mass and energy are two forms of the same thing. Energy is liberated matter, and matter is energy waiting to happen. Energy is trapped within every living thing, and every living thing is nothing but dense energy patterns. Recently scientists put subatomic particles into a 'collider' and discovered that there is no source for the energy. Apparently the energy moves so fast that it cannot be measured. Things only look solid to the naked eye, as the particles vibrate slower than the speed of light. So we perceive things as being solid, but actually we are all vibrating, dancing particles of energy.

Many people are able to feel this energy. As you begin to work with the subtle energies of the universe and start meditating, you will evolve, and you will vibrate at a different frequency. If you could actually measure your own energy field when you are feeling low or depressed, you would find that your particles vibrate at a slower rate. When you are happy and grateful, you vibrate at a higher level; you will be 'buzzing', so to speak.

You will also vibrate at a higher frequency after taking exercise, especially yoga or tai chi. Sound also enhances the frequency of vibrating particles. If you are familiar with sound therapy, you will understand that different cells in the body have different frequencies and can be affected by different musical tones. The use of tuning forks in therapies is now more widely accepted, but for those of you who have not yet had the pleasure of sound therapy, a gong bath, chakra sound therapy, or an alignment with singing bowls, just think of how music can affect the body and emotions. Some music will bring stillness within the soul, while other tunes and melodies will make you want to dance and be happy. Think about it: this isn't a new idea. It's just being brought to the forefront, and I am so grateful that I can be part of this awakening.

If you take a tuning fork into a room with other tuning forks all calibrated to different frequencies, and ding the one you are holding, any other calibrated to the same frequency as yours will also ding. Like forces attract like. If you are feeling happy and joyous, you will attract happiness. If you are feeling sad, the same applies. Think of how you can feel 'drawn down' when you are in the presence of lower-frequency people. There is nothing wrong with this. We all vibrate differently, and remember, we are all here to have experiences, so some days you will feel amazing while on others life will have dealt you a wild card, and you may feel low or sad. Remember when this happens that you can use your mindfulness exercises and think about how you are feeling and what created it. From that space of mindfulness, using your breath, you can decide if it is truly important, and you can decide to respond to how you feel.

This is a time when our world is being realigned with the more subtle threads of the universe. This is a time of connecting and re-alising our true purpose and how we are all connected. Once again, thank heavens for those scientists. People are now beginning to 'get it'!

Please excuse that little moment of 'woo woo', but I'm breaking you in gently!

Try this little exercise from energy pioneer Donna Eden:

- Take a moment to settle and take a few breaths.
- Bring your palms towards each other, as if you were going to clap, but stop three inches before your hands make contact.
- Now twist your wrists so your arms form an *X*. The wrists should be at the centre, still three inches apart.

- Draw your attention to the space between your wrists. They contain several energy centres, and these energies will connect. You should feel some sensation in the area between them.
- Try moving your wrists an inch closer and then back. See what you can feel.

Present-moment awareness is an essential part of manifesting. You need to create a feeling of deep gratitude for what you already have and an awareness of the fact that you already have exactly what you need. This is not an easy process if you have never thought about this before, but take your time. Use some mindful breath work and begin to realise exactly what you have gratitude for. You may not have that dream job or that big house, but you can feel the gratitude for the sunshine and the roof over your head, the food you have eaten, and the family you may have.

Yoga and breath work are a good place to start. Taking time out and just being, feeling, and enjoying. *Life.* We are evolving on an energetic level unlike anything we have ever known. We are present in exciting times.

The basics for manifesting include having a clear idea of what you want to achieve, believing you will achieve it, and adding strong positive emotional energy to the process. Once you have the idea, belief, and emotion, combine them into an image and release the image with the expectation that on the higher dimension of creation, it is done. The words you use are very important. If you state, 'I want…' the universe will give you exactly that—the *wanting*. Timing is also essential. Be specific. The universe likes specifics. Set your intention with a date—for example, 'By December 2015, I will have been on a weekend break to Rome with my husband.'

The better you can do this, the more successful you'll be at manifesting. People who have taken Reiki level two with me will learn one technique; others use a 'dream board', while some use crystal grids and pendulums, as I teach in Reiki master healer workshops. Just writing a list of your intentions will make your desires 'real', and there are lots of books on the subject. One of the easiest to begin with is *The Secret*, by Rhonda Byrne. If you can, purchase the DVD as well. It makes the book an easier read! Some of you will say this is a very materialistic book. I say it is a good place to start.

Find your way.

You will be amazed.

The biggest tip I can give you is to be specific with your words. I learnt this the long way round.

I had always wanted a Jaguar XKR. The key word there is 'wanted'. A client of mine owned one. I loved the shape, and I loved how she looked when she emerged from it. It was always my dream car. I never really believed I would ever own one. This was fifteen years ago. The car was way out of my league! This was in the early days, before I expanded and developed the two large salons. This was also before I became 'connected' and developed energetically and spiritually. On those trips out when I maybe passed one, or came across one in a car park, I would always admire it. It was always the 'dream'.

When you actively start to use manifesting in your life, the words you use are very important. If you say, as the car of your dreams passes you on the motorway, 'I've always wanted one of those', the universe gives you that—the wanting of it. You must be very specific! I learnt this early on.

About a year before my birthday, I wrote on a dream board with a photograph of the dream car, 'On my fortieth birthday, I will have a Jaguar XKR.'

I understood that I really needed to feel the car and was desperate to test-drive one. My husband thought I was mad. Then one day, under duress, he accompanied me to a Jag dealership and we test-drove one 'for fun'. I think he did it to keep me quiet, but I was in the zone, and off I went! I needed to feel what it was like. Bizarrely, I fell in love with the

sound of the indicator! My lovely husband got on board with the process and we took a brochure home with us. This was used to add some more colour to the dream board.

For Christmas that year, he bought me a Jaguar key ring that I put my Volvo keys on. Every time I got in the Volvo, I felt it was the Jag, in every part of me. I could hear the indicator and smell the leather. I then began to forget about my plan. It's like sowing seeds: you plant them, water them, and then let them grow. You have to relinquish your need to know what they will grow into. In manifesting, you have to relinquish the need to know *how* you will achieve your desire.

Remember the exact words I used on the dream board? My fortieth birthday arrived, and I got exactly what I asked for: a Jaguar XKR for the day! My lovely husband had organised a surprise twenty-four-hour test drive for me! I had been specific. I had got exactly that! I should have put, 'By my fortieth birthday, I will *own* a Jaguar XKR!'

So be careful what you wish for. You will always get it! However, the day out gave us the insight that no matter how much money we ever had, we didn't want a brand-new one, and we didn't want a convertible like we had borrowed. So it wasn't a wasted manifestation. It taught me a great deal.

Eighteen months later, having moved house, I sold the salons and reworded my dream board. Then my husband came home from a trip away and stated that 'the universe had spoken to him'. Now, if you knew my husband, you would know he was the most unspiritual-manifesting boy you could get, with a military background and an 'if you can't see it, then it can't be real' attitude. As you can imagine, the news that he had received a lightbulb moment or some divine intervention was a bit of a shock! To be honest, I had forgotten about the car plan, and I was busy setting up my new business. It was the last thing on my mind, but the seed was still sown.

He had found my dream car, he said. Exact colour, age, and model. We bought her. And I enjoyed every moment. She was exactly as I had remembered from the test drive. Every time I drove her I felt such gratitude for her and the manifesting process. After a while, due to her age, her upkeep costs began to escalate and we decided to sell her before we fell out of love with her. I decided to move on and manifest a replacement. Using the same process of test driving and feeling that I was driving a different car I was able to purchase a lovely little Mini Cooper S, again the exact model, colour, and age I had manifested. I didn't compromise on anything, and although this time we had both been on board with looking, we'd found it tricky to sell my beloved Jag. So I had to sit back and trust, and when I least expected it, a new client walked across the drive, admired the car, and within two weeks bought her. I couldn't believe it. Sometimes pushing and pushing for what you want just doesn't work. You have to be proactive by putting adverts in and setting the intention to sell, but you then have to trust that all your needs will be met.

Now, there are some little 'clauses' to add to this manifesting lark. Some people will say that it's not all about material things. I agree, but this was the best story to show you how word-specific you have to be. I could have told you about how my business sold, how my husband always manages to be off shift at Christmas, how certain clients just turn up when I think about them—but the car has been the best learning curve in the rules of manifesting for me. Sometimes, though, no matter how much you want something, the universe has a different plan, a plan that you cannot change, and often it is a plan with an outcome that is far better than your original dream. Only when you receive that ultimate gift will you see how the web of manifesting mysteries all link together.

Start here:

- Practice your mindful breathing daily and begin to notice how you are feeling. Notice the emotions that are present, but try not to become consumed by the woe-is-me syndrome. Notice and accept.
- Make some quiet time for yourself and create a dream board of the things you wish to create. Take time with your wording. Remember the universe needs specifics: dates, times, etc.

- Place the dream board somewhere you can see it, but leave it there. You have sown the seed. Now let it develop.
- Feel that you already have the things you desire. This is the most difficult part of the process for many, but remember the story of the car. Feel it. Test-drive it. Smell it. And believe it with all your being.
- Give up your need to know *how* you will receive your manifested dreams. We always believe that it revolves around money and the fact that we don't think we have enough to purchase the item of our desires. It's not all about the money: you may be gifted something or, you may win it. Give up the need to know how. Just feel it.

EMBRACE THE FEAR

Most of your fears never come true. Whatever little scenarios you have mapped out in your mind about the 'what ifs' are a complete waste of time, and most importantly a waste of energy. But without fear, we would not be human. As spiritual beings in human bodies, we are meant to be experiencing things. I was accused many years ago of having an unhealthy need to be happy all the time. I thought this rather odd and actually took great offence when it was said to me. I was disappointed by the thought that maybe I had got it all wrong and maybe I was meant to be sad. Then I realised we are not meant to be one way or the other. We just are.

Everything is exactly as it is meant to be. Emotions are part of being human, and these emotions shape our lives and personalities. Some people will always be born worriers while others will always have the luck faerie following them around, and some will be living in poverty while others will have ill health. This is as it is. I have seen many clients in my career who I wished I could change. I wished they could see the bigger picture and switch their thoughts or take that plunge. It used to frustrate me so much until I had a lightbulb moment and realised that if we were all the same and 'got it', the world would be quite a boring place, with us all being on exactly the same path. The delightful part of being human is that we are all different.

Some people will go through their whole lives happy and content with their lot and not wishing for anything more. To others these people may seem to be stuck and needing more. Just because we don't all want the same things doesn't mean that we are in the wrong place. Remember, there is no such thing as right or wrong. Things just are. Accept people for what they are. If someone needs help in finding his or her way, then we can help him or her. Timing is a big part of the journey, and trust is an even bigger part. Trust is something you can't really explain. Trust is a feeling. It's not really tangible. It is an experience.

I learnt about trust when I was trying to sell my two salons. Back in 2006 I had sold my Ilminster salon subject to contract, and my Taunton one was on the market. We were buying a beautiful house on the north side of town, about two miles away, that was owned by friends of mine. There was a barn behind the property that we had got planning permission to turn into a lovely therapy room. It was all systems go. I just needed to sell first, but I had been told by a client who was used to buying businesses that the Taunton salon wouldn't sell, as I was still working in it.

Ilminster sold immediately, as I'd had it running as a separate entity. I was only there once a week to collect takings and check that everything was okay with the staff. I treated a few clients there, but nothing like the numbers I saw in the Taunton salon. My client's advice was to put a manageress in at Taunton and step back. Then a potential buyer would see that if I left, I would not be taking clients with me. The salon would be running on its own, without me. Until then, after building the business for eighteen years, I had been known as 'Nicki at Genesis'. I *was* the business.

Taking this advice on board, I decided to implement changes—halfheartedly, mind you. After all, I was scared. I was fearful that if I stepped away, I would lose my income, and I was the main earner within the salon. If the takings reduced, I wouldn't be able to live, let alone sell up. This would be disaster! Sheer panic! So I went for the half measure. I employed a part time manageress, with the view that she would take over when I sold. She had great experience in the industry, and I trusted her on a management level. Bringing fresh blood in meant I wasn't emotionally swayed by promoting someone within the existing team.

We had issues, though. The staff didn't really like her. I had potential bullying issues arising, and I had more stress building than I had bargained for. I hadn't really listened to the advice I was given. Well, I had listened, and I had chosen to take my own path. I had made a choice. The events that followed really tested me.

A few days before my husband and I left for a ski holiday, our vendors pulled out. They decided that they didn't want to move after all. I was astounded. To make things worse on an emotional level, these friends had chosen to tell me alone. The wife met me for a coffee one afternoon in town. I thought we were meeting to organise the survey, and I had no idea of what was to come. She said they were back pedaling. They didn't want to move. The conversation became a bit of a blur, like you see in films: words being spoken, the room becoming muffled, my heart pounding. Sheer fear and panic consumed me. She was obviously nervous about telling me the news, unsure of my response.

I breathed. I drew upon my knowledge as a healer. I said the right things. I said I understood. I said she must do what was right for her and that the sale had to be right for all parties. I think she was a bit shocked that I took it so well. She paid for the drinks and left. I went to the toilet and burst into tears. My whole body was shaking and I didn't know what to do. My world was in a spin and I needed to focus. The first thing was to call my husband, who was working in Ireland at the time. How on earth could I tell him? He knew I was having the meeting, so I think he had a feeling from my squeaky voice that something wasn't quite right. He was angry—very angry. Thank heavens he was a thousand miles away. By the time he arrived home, we had calmed down and begun to see the bigger picture.

A few days later we left for our ski trip. I used my 'switch your thoughts' training to turn what seemed like the end of our dream right around. We discussed that it was all meant to be. We knew that there was a better property out there, and we talked about what had made me the most angry and upset. The most upsetting part was that our friends had not had the courage to tell us together. It was just her and me, not the four of us. But that was their choice. It happened. It had passed. Now what were we going to do? We had to move on.

We were skiing in Austria, staying in the most fabulous hotel with a stunning spa. Sitting by the fire pit in the afternoon of our first day, we began creating new ideas of where we could go. We thought positive thoughts and started to enjoy our holiday. Then disaster struck. On the second day I broke my wrist. Not only did I break it, I dislocated it. I have never felt pain like it. The superb medical team popped it back into place and put a plaster cast on, and the rest of the holiday was spent very, very bored. I had plenty of time to think.

Sometimes when you don't take notice of warning signs or advice, the universe will come along and give you a wake-up call. This was mine. I hadn't broken my leg, which was a blessing, as I lived in the flat above the salon and had a dog to walk, so on a practical level I was thankful for that. Being incapacitated for a while did, however, show me so much.

I couldn't work for eight weeks. No clients for two whole months. During this time, the client who had offered me the advice of stepping away from the salon came forward and made me an offer. The universe works in mysterious ways, and after giving up my attachment to 'how' I was going to sell, things just fell into place. Originally he had only been interested in the property. It wasn't really a business he had wanted to get into, and who really knows what changed his mind, but I was thankful. I was immensely thankful, although it had taken a painful injury to get there.

If I hadn't been out of the salon for those two months, it would have been a different story. He wouldn't have seen that it didn't fall apart without me, and he wouldn't have bought it. He now also knew that as the property we were purchasing had fallen through, and as it had been only two miles away, he could now stipulate a wider radius clause in the contract, therefore safeguarding the client base he was going to purchase. Otherwise there would have been an issue with me working too close to the new day spa he was building.

I had already started to look further afield for property, and therefore I had more choice. Who knew what was going to happen? The eight weeks of free time gave me space to trawl the estate agents and look for new premises. It gave me the chance to have coffees with friends and take longer walks with the dog. It made me learn about patience. I learnt to ask people to tie my shoelaces, and to accept help packing bags in the supermarket. I learnt to write with my left hand, and I learnt that it didn't matter that it took me twice as long to get dressed in the morning, as I actually had all day! It didn't matter that unloading the dishwasher took an age with one hand, and that I had to ask my husband to do the ironing.

I had time. Time to overthink.

With this time my mind would run riot. There was excitement that the salon was under offer, but also fear that I didn't have anywhere to go. Panic, panic… What to do? The properties we were viewing were all wrong. The intercity train was running past one we viewed; another was on a blind bend with no parking. I began to get very depressed. Then one of those energy-shifting lightbulb moments came along when I was talking to a client about my

concerns over the search for new premises. Her words were, 'Nicki, I don't care if you treat me in a field. POW! Trust—I needed to trust. It really didn't matter where I worked. I realised the 'worst' case would be that we could rent a house for a while, and I could work as a mobile therapist until we found somewhere permanent. Not ideal, but at least I could keep clients and still have an income. The very next day, our dream property was in the local paper—so fresh on the market that there were no printed details. We viewed it that afternoon and put an offer in the next day. It was accepted.

If our friends hadn't pulled out of the sale, our buyer wouldn't have been so keen to purchase, as I would have been working too close to him. If I hadn't broken my wrist, I wouldn't have backed away and let the salon run itself. I learnt to feel my emotions. I felt fear. I felt anger. I certainly felt pain! Then, I learnt trust. I moved beyond the fear.

So when people were saying, 'Oh, how awful for you to have broken your wrist!' I could say, 'It was the most painful thing ever, but it was one of the best things that ever happened to me.'

Take a moment and look at the bigger picture

- Accept where you are. You may not like it, but accept it. Be mindful of it.

- Trust. The hardest thing of all. When you realise how to trust and let go, amazing things happen.

- Stop overanalysing. Stop getting yourself into the 'why me' syndrome. It serves no purpose, but just takes you round in a self-pitying circle. Stop it. It wastes energy. Remember this.

- Feel the fear and move beyond it. We are meant to have feelings. Acknowledge them. Understand what has made you feel this way and choose what to do about it.

Feel the fear and decide what to do with it. Start with the breath, and develop trust.

Taking that step is one of the hardest things. I'm not talking about bungee jumping or tackling that black run. It could be anything. It could be speaking your truth and letting your family know how you feel about certain things. It could be a deeper, more spiritual need to take a step. It could have to do with travelling, or with changing a job. All these things are connected. With breath work, mindfulness, and manifesting, you may find you have to face the fear.

Face the fear and move on.

Within the energetic map of your body, deep within the chakras, is your fear centre, the control centre that is the solar plexus chakra, or, to give it its Sanskrit name, Manipura. It's the yellow one—you know, the one above the sacral and beneath the heart.

The one that gets missed out. The one that you feel those butterflies in when you are nervous, or the one that creates tightness within your diaphragm, giving your lungs nowhere to expand and making your breath short and your pulse race.

It is ruled by the element of fire, and it purifies toxicity on all levels. It gives us fuel that we need to put things into action, and gives strength and vitality, bringing the elements of the two lower chakras into being. The solar plexus chakra is the place where your ego resides. The power from this chakra will enable your true purpose to manifest. Your ego is part of you, and I believe that we need to acknowledge our individuality and therefore be aware of our egos. So many teachers try to squash the ego. I spent years being aware and every time it popped up, trying to squash it.

'You shouldn't let your ego get in the way', I was told. But I am human. Everyone has an ego. We have personalities and therefore egos. Surely we should be just be aware of them, at least, and notice when they begin to get in the way of our path or development. When the ego is healthy, it is connected to the creator source and uses the energy that comes in from the higher chakras manifesting love, creation, and divine will. It brings together the energies of the chakras below that form our grounded development, to enable us to function at our most creative. If your solar plexus chakra is underactive and out of balance, it can cause feelings of weakness, despair, and 'why me' syndrome. If overactive, it can make you feel aggressive, controlling, arrogant, and short-tempered.

Connecting and focusing through this chakra is so important. We are often busy asking for energy to flow through the crown into the heart, and in the case of Reiki, giving from your heart space. We then feel too spaced out and 'away with the faeries', so we start to draw our attention to the root chakra, by grounding to Mother Earth and feeling the earthy energies of the planet. We forget that these two areas are all manifesting in the solar plexus.

It's the place that makes us feel fearful, the space that gives us butterflies, and the space that makes us feel like someone has punched us when our world looks like it could fall apart. Focus on it. Visualise it. Meditate on it. It is your friend. The central chakra is there to guide you.

The ego holds power, and the ego has the power to choose

This chakra is the centre of all your fears. It's where you develop trust, but first you must master the breath. Feel the breath as you did in chapter four.

WHAT ARE THESE CHAKRA THINGS?

Following my experience with the solar plexus chakra and my ego, after having my massage with Phil in Braunton, I visited my acupuncturist ready to tell her of my 'findings'. She understood, but apparently, in Chinese medicine, they don't work with the chakras. Silly me, of course. They work with meridians and the flow of energy with pools called the Dantian and Hara points—, not actual chakras. The use of chakra energy within healing is a vast subject that is not used by everyone, but most people have seen an image of these energy centres. Haven't they? Pictures in yoga magazines and meditative images surround us, but as with many 'New Age' things, we find them when we are ready. There must have been a time in my life that I first discovered them, so there must have been a time when I too was unaware. The time of the switch eludes me, as I feel I have always known about them, but I am aware when I talk to clients that not everyone knows what they are. They may have seen images, but have little or no knowledge of the uses or of what happens when areas are out of balance.

Most people who practice yoga have seen images of them, but they may not realise how useful they can be in healing the body and understanding 'blockages'. What exactly are they? What do we 'do' with them? Some people pop into conversations, 'Oh, your throat chakra may be blocked.' Is it? Are you afraid to ask what they mean?

So here is a little master class just for you. This is a vast subject, and many reading this may already know about the beautiful spinning wheels of the chakra energy system, but equally many may not. After all, this is a book of explanation of the woo woo! This is not an in-depth chapter that will leave you boggled. There are many other books and courses available for that!

Remember, you are made up of energy. We have already established this; it can be measured, and some people can actually see it. The aura is an egg-shaped energy field surrounding the body and has the ability to expand and contract, depending on how 'energised' you are. You will find that you will have a more 'full' aura after exercise, meditation, or yoga, whereas if you are unwell or sad, your aura will contract. Sometimes when you enter a room you feel yourself drawn to one person; this is due to his or her aura extending outwards and you being drawn to something within it. Like attracting like. It's something you 'resonate' with, and likewise your aura will contract when you sense something wrong or when you talk to someone who maybe has a more 'negative' energy. You recoil as a form of energetic protection.

The aura contains all the seven colours of the rainbow, the full spectrum of light, as does the system of chakras. The first layer is closest to the body and is the densest in vibration. The layers become lighter and faster in their vibration the farther away from the body they are. Some people can see an aura, while some people may feel it. When I give Reiki treatments and other energy work, I am aware of how far the energetic body is extending from my client, but I have never seen colours. As the aura is an energetic field that is electromagnetic in nature, it can be photographed using new technology imaging, and this is a fantastic way to show people that they have more than just a physical body.

When there is a disturbance in our energy field and our energy centres are out of balance, disease and disharmony can occur on a physical or emotional level. It is becoming more and apparent that as a human race we are evolving at a high speed and are beginning to realise that emotions cause physical effects within the body. Stress and depression can cause all sorts of physical ailments. This is why more and more people are beginning to take their emotional health much more seriously and are embracing yoga, meditation, and thankfully, as you saw in chapter four, mindfulness.

In the grand scheme of things, little is really known about the chakras. They originate from the Hindu tradition, and the word translates from Sanskrit as 'wheel', although according to Wikipedia, a yogic translation is 'vortex' or 'whirlpool'. As in Chinese medicines the acupuncture points feel like little vortexes where the needles actually get drawn in, it seems rather appropriate to visualise chakras in a similar way, rather than just as spinning wheels. After all, we are three-dimensional beings.

As each chakra resonates to the colours of the rainbow, they are quite easy to remember, although I have to admit I have never felt the need to learn the Sanskrit names for each one. They also resonate to the musical scale of C, which is why certain points within this system can be affected by different types of music and why sound therapy using crystal bowls and tuning forks can be a wonderful way of creating balance within the body. C is the root and B is the crown. So if you wish to work with rebalancing and aligning your throat chakra, you will need a tuning fork or crystal bowl that resonates to G. If you sing, which I don't, you will be able to 'sound' yourself. Sing a perfect G, and if it wobbles or sounds cracked, keep allowing the sound to move through your body and it will change to the correct pitch as the chakra balances. This is an easy way of using sound therapy on yourself, but it is best done when you are peaceful, having just completed some meditation or yoga.

Some people say that the chakras develop within the energetic body as a person grows in age, with each having a seven-year cycle.

For instance, from birth to the age of seven, our root chakra is developing, while from eight to fourteen, our sacral chakra develops, and so on. This means that our chakras are not fully developed until we are in our forties. Other people believe that our chakras are all developed by the time we are in our twenties, and that we just need to give attention to each one to keep them energised and healthy. Some people will, on their pathway, never be aware of these funny vortexes at all, but others will evolve as 'enlightened' beings and need to focus more on different chakras, depending on how their life path unfolds. For instance, someone who has recently been bereaved will find their heart chakra is out of balance and in need of nourishment in the way of heartfelt healing. Others who have problems communicating or who have persistent coughs or sore throats may have to look towards their throat chakra for balance.

It's all really about noticing, becoming aware, and creating balance, and as I have said before, this can be done by meditation, yoga, or seeking help through a variety of healing modalities, such as Reiki or colour therapy. There are many guided chakra meditations available that can help you rebalance and heal. If a chakra is out of balance for someone, you might see him or her wearing a crystal of a specific colour to bring about healing. The wearing of a specific colour will also help. You may have also seen yoga blankets for *Savasana* (relaxation at the end of a session) in the colours of the rainbow. These help to rebalance and help you focus on the full chakra system. Similarly, you can purchase chakra beads, bracelets, and candles. I have a full range of chakra candles which all have a different blend of essential oils within them, which I can burn during treatments and which clients can purchase to use at home—obviously not burning all at the same time!

Just as colours resonate to the chakras, so do oils and crystals. You will find that you are drawn to certain healing techniques at different times in your life. Experiment with the tools you have. I like to use the technique of dowsing with a pendulum over chakras to ascertain if they are balanced, and then I use Reiki to treat the ones that are out of balance. However, I usually find that after most treatments that I offer, the energetic field and chakras will naturally rebalance, and when checked at the end of the session will show as balanced and energised.

You can delve even further into gemstones that resonate with different chakras and how each one affects another, especially through healing, but for now, here is a basic explanation of the colours and emotions held within these powerful areas.

For me, when I feel an emotional issue that needs addressing, I take a moment and check in with my body and how it feels. I notice where any tightness or restrictive sensations may be, and I focus on the centre that may be blocked or out of balance. Sometimes just visualising the colour of that energy centre growing brighter and brighter is all that is needed, while other times I can move this energy during a yoga class or during exercise.

I became very aware of how much we need to pay attention to our solar plexus chakra after a trip to North Devon in terrible traffic that nearly made me late. I was on my way to see the amazing Phil for a massage and found myself getting more and more anxious. The roads were terribly congested. Not only was the traffic not helping, but I also took a wrong turn which made me even more anxious. I'm never late! I normally arrive at least half an hour early so I can find a parking space and have a coffee prior to arriving at the therapy centre. Today was not to be one of those organised days.

Having changed my lifestyle and career path seven years prior to this, I had become distanced from the feeling of anxiety and stress. The palpitations in my body and my sheer panic that I would be late, or worse, not arrive at all, were consuming me. You would think that having a massage to calm and soothe after a trip like I had would be a good thing? Today I was going to experience something quite different.

I can honestly say, I've had a few lightbulb changing moments in my time. Most being during treatments where I have found profound shifts take place. This was one of them. Normally I go for an unraveling treatment where Phil uses a mixture of techniques including deep tissue massage, reiki, and fascial release. I book for 90 minutes to make it worth the very long drive, but today he had to cut my treatment short. Apparently, to quote Phil 'I'm stopping here as your body can't take any more. Your solar plexus is shot to pieces.' That sounds quite blunt, but that was the defining moment, and we did have chance for more chat and discussions after I had dressed.

For anyone who has ever experienced an energetic shift, you will know that it is not always pleasant. This wasn't pleasant at all and I was left very angry that I had allowed myself to get in to that state in the first place. Just think for a moment. The drive and my lack of control over the journey and traffic had started to affect my control centre. My solar plexus. My breathing was affected and the tightness under my ribs was getting worse, but I had failed to check in early enough to deal with it.

It was no doubt an accumulation of other things that combined together to make an even bigger issue. I was due to go skiing a few weeks later and I'm sure that my annual fear that I need to ski faster to be able to ski better, wasn't helping! Thankfully from a treatment point of view, it was noticed and we were able to deal with it. But the bigger picture was the realisation that the solar plexus chakra is often overlooked. In experiencing this first hand I was able to understand the need to pay more attention to it.

To my amazement the even bigger picture was that chapter six was almost written in my head on the way home. I had been stuck at chapter five and had been for a few weeks, so thank you universe for providing me with another awesome experience. One that I can share and enable people to see how valuable these chakra centres can be. I needed to pull mindfulness techniques into place earlier than I did, but if I had, the treatment would have been different and this chapter would have been written in a different way.

Remember, things are exactly as they are meant to be.

Notice your emotions. Notice how your body feels.

You are allowed to *feel*. You are human.

The Basic Map of the Chakras

Root – Red

(Muladhara)

Situated at the base of the spine, it connects us with the essence of the earth, maintaining our stability, patience, and physical survival.

Sacral – Orange

(Svadisthana)

Sometimes referred to as the naval chakra, this centre generates energies within our sexual centre, stimulating new ideas, creativity, passion, and endurance.

Solar Plexus – Yellow

(Manipura)

Just below the rib cage, this is the area in which you experience 'butterflies' when anxious or nervous. This centre is where fear is held. Personal power, identity, and personality, together with your inner glow, can be found here.

Heart – Green

(Anahta)

Found in the centre of the chest, it is your 'heart space' and contains your emotional centre for promoting compassion, love, understanding, and most importantly, forgiveness.

Throat – Blue

(Visuddha)

The area of communication and self-expression. Often an area that becomes blocked when heartfelt issues are not expressed with either the voice or with the arms and hands.

Third Eye – Indigo

(Ajna)

Located between the brows, it is a centre linked to your inner connection with source, your intuition, and psychic abilities.

Crown – Violet/Purple

(Sahasrara)

Found at the top of the head, it is a centre for inspiration and imagination. This area is responsible for our spiritual well-being. The energy from source comes through the

crown to the rest of the chakras.

REIKI FOUND ME!

Many years ago I had an amazing therapist working with me. Jo was rather special in more ways than one. Not only was she a superb beauty therapist, but we had a kind of telepathic connection. We never needed to finish our sentences to each other; we just knew what each other required. I trusted her implicitly with my salon, and she was my right-hand woman! Jo had a shoulder injury from an old riding accident and was finding the amount of leg waxing that we did during the summer quite demanding on her body. These were the days back in the early

1990s, when we were more of a beauty salon. Waxing made up a vast amount of our trade, especially during the warmer months.

Day spas and such like had not evolved at that time, and Jo was with me when I first discovered Repechage at a trade show. We were looking for a treatment where we could help the client detox with an all-over body treatment. The only one on the market was Dead Sea Minerals, and that was already in a local salon. The most 'spa-like' you could get was a body scrub followed by a massage. This was the time well before gel nails weren't invented and French polish was very new and exciting!

Although Jo was with me when we introduced this line to the salon, she still found the waxing treatments were taking their toll on her body, so she decided to go and learn Reiki. I had no idea what this strange thing was. She had always held an interest in crystals and healing. This was her path. Her path unfolded in front of her, and in 1996 she left me! I was devastated. She left to start up a business of her own, where waxing was limited and Reiki took precedence. We kept in touch but grew apart.

During the next few years, my own salon developed. Repechage and its seaweed treatments became my main product line, and the spa industry started to evolve. More staff joined the team, and new premises had to be found. I had become very interested in La Stone therapy, which is an amazing massage therapy using hot and cold stones to rebalance the body and mind. I desperately wanted to train in this new therapy that had been brought into the UK from Tucson in Arizona. My holistic side was developing even more, and although it wasn't a prerequisite to the course, I felt that I needed to learn Reiki before embarking on this new treatment.

Reiki is a strange word that no one knows how to pronounce—until it finds you! Reiki, pronounced 'ray key', is one of those things you may have heard of or seen written or even received a treatment for, or you may have absolutely no idea what I am talking about. Remember back to chapter five which explained a little about how we are all vibrating with particles of energy? Well, Reiki is just a way of using and channeling this energy with its origins being from Japan. Translated, Reiki means 'universal energy', the life-force energy that resides within every being on the planet—every atom, every molecule.

Rei is the Japanese word meaning *universal,* and is also a reference to the higher dimension of light and the soul.

Ki means *vital life-force energy* which interpenetrates and connects all.

I needed to find someone to train me and several years had passed since Jo had moved on. She had become a Reiki master and was therefore able to teach and pass on her knowledge. I called her. 'I've waited seven years for you to get off your bum and call me for this', she said. Well, timing is everything, after all!

Certain events then unfolded that I wouldn't really understand the reason for until a few years later. Jo told me she was unable to teach me, as she was intending to go travelling for a year. This was not really what I wanted to hear, but she sent me to her Reiki master. I went on trust. A big step. But trust, as we have previously seen, is a powerful thing.

My Reiki master for level one and two was a lady called Fran from Newton Abbot. I took my Reiki one and then level two within a month, as I wanted to have both of these qualifications before attending my La Stone course that was already booked. I approached Reiki like another qualification. I did my homework and received my certificates in a very organised and pragmatic way. I expected thunderbolts and lightning to come from my palms and for my life to change. But nothing happened. Well, nothing dynamic and profound. It was all rather subtle. Clients who were receiving massage therapy from me were commenting on the different 'feel' of things. I found the distance healing with Reiki rather bizarre and difficult to grasp, until I was nudged to use it to send Reiki ahead of me to my La Stone course. I was anxious about embarking on five days training away from home and Jo suggested that I send Reiki ahead of me to be there every day when I was training. It would give me empowerment and a sense of calm. This is how powerful Reiki can be. Amazing! Why didn't everyone do this? Reiki needed to be given to more people, and I was exploding with the need to spread the word. I began to use it with all my treatments, if clients wanted it.

Jo never did go travelling. The universe had a plan for me. At the time of taking my first two Reiki levels, I had no intention of teaching or even progressing to the level of master healer. I just wanted to be able to use energy in a more structured way. I wanted the piece of paper and I really, *really* wanted to do the La Stone. I wasn't to know that within five years I too would be teaching, and my path would have changed directions completely.

During those five years, I would be sending many clients to Jo so they too could learn. I soon realised that clients wanted me to teach them. I approached Jo to take me through the next two levels, and the lightbulb once again was switched on. I had the privilege of having two masters, so I could see two very different teaching styles. This enabled me to develop my own unique way. How perfect was that? I designed my own course, keeping the traditions of Reiki but adding my own twist and modern feel. I realised that it should be taught to not only those wanting to treat clients as a business, but to those looking to understand the subtle workings of energy through the body and how they could utilise it for self-healing. I began teaching in 2006.

One of the reasons for selling my two salons was that I was unable to teach during the week, as the salon was busy and I required a peaceful space where students could focus and have a truly memorable day. Teaching on Sundays was not ideal, and I found it very tiring. It was time to sell up and change direction.

Not everyone wants to learn to channel Reiki themselves, many find it an ideal way to receive healing within a salon environment, without actively looking for the more woo woo side of things. Some will come to me for a facial and receive Reiki during the hour treatment which will enhance the way they feel, giving them that extra balance and relaxation. Ailments can be treated and emotional imbalances causing stress can be reduced through Reiki. It can also help greatly with the removal of toxins from chemotherapy and anaesthesia. It is unconditional healing for the body and mind and will flow to wherever it is needed within the body. It is always given for the 'highest good' of the recipient, with this beautiful energy being a gentle way of enabling self-healing and the healing of others, pets, and even food and plants. The possibilities are endless, and the more people that are attuned to this gentle but powerful energy, the healthier and more calm we will all become, able to deal with our everyday lives much more easily.

You may have seen the word Reiki alongside these two *kanji*—written characters—for Reiki are extremely common in Japan and can be found in a variety of situations unrelated to the word 'Reiki'. They were often used in the teachings of Reiki. The name of them merely meant 'spiritual energy'. It was only when Reiki came to the West that the actual word 'Reiki' turned into the name for the system. The original aim of these teachings back in the early 1900s was to provide a method for students to achieve enlightenment. Unlike in a religion, there was no belief system attached, and enlightenment was the aim. The healing

霊

気

that took place was merely secondary, and in the very beginning there was no distinction between people wishing to be healed and students wanting to be taught.

Reiki is such a beautiful energy. It is so safe and self-replenishing that it is the perfect place to start when you begin to explore the subtle workings of the universe. Anyone can be attuned to channeling this energy, and some people choose to embark on training and only use it for themselves, for self-healing. Some take it further and want to teach themselves or use it in their life path for healing others, but you may still want to know what attunements are. And what are these strange symbols people talk about?

Attunements are unique and powerful processes wherein a student is reconnected with the flow of this beautiful light energy. I don't like to call it a ceremony, as people then think it will be some incense-burning, wand-wielding process where we all chant. It isn't—thankfully! If it were, I would have been put off years ago. It is a beautiful, unique experience and powerful healing in its own right, which is why you must choose your Reiki master wisely. Or, more often, like the old saying, 'When the student is ready, the master will appear.'

There is so much to learn, books to read and people to meet. Reiki has changed my life and I had no idea of the direction it would take me. After all, that path was originally taken so I could attend my La Stone course. Funny old place, this universe of ours.

MAKING ASSUMPTIONS IS A WASTE OF TIME

We all do it. We all have felt the 'what if' and the 'why did they do that?' emotions. We are, after all, human. I know I keep saying it, but we are, and I see how the energy given to the making of assumptions diminishes the light held within people. I see how human beings spend a great deal of time worrying about things they have no control over, and how people can cause ill feeling within others with a simple misuse of words.

There is an amazing little book that you may have come across, *The Four Agreements*, by Don Miguel Ruiz. I forget how I found it, but it changed my way of looking at things. It changed the way I related to my clients, and it certainly made me look very closely at how words are used.

Very often the emotions created by words spoken are felt long after the words are forgotten.

There is no point in me rewriting Don Miguel's book here in a simple form, but I can condense the meaning as I see it. These four very simple 'agreements' can really help you use your energy wisely and direct your thoughts in a different way. This will enable you to move through your life a little freer and able to literally see things differently. Remember, though, that not everyone is evolving at the same speed as you. Everyone is on a different path, and some people will always be negative and ready to blame others. You can spend a lifetime trying to change people and make them see things the way you do, but I have learnt that you can only take a horse to water; you cannot make it drink. Frustrating as it may be, you can only do your best. You cannot force people against their will to change or to see it your way, and sometimes you have to step back to just allow them to find a path that suits them. Everyone has free will and has to make their choices. Remember that there is no such thing as right or wrong. What may be right for you may be wrong for another. Be respectful of one another's choices. **The Four Agreements:**

1) **Be impeccable with your word.**

2) **Don't take things personally.**

3) **Don't make assumptions.**

4) **Always do your best.**

One of the biggest assumptions I made in my life was *assuming* that people would think I had failed when I decided to sell my businesses. I worried, I procrastinated, and I delayed. I put far too much energy into worrying about what others would think. With hindsight, that was such a waste of time and energy, but at the time it was how I felt, and what other people thought meant a great deal.

It wasn't until I took that leap of faith and decided that I wanted a different path that I realised not one client was thinking what I had presumed they would. In fact, the client that said, 'Nicki, I don't care if you treat me in a field', gave me a real lightbulb moment. It made me realise that I had absolutely no idea what other people thought. I needed to take a moment and settle. I needed to see what I had, to be grateful for what I had created and who I was, and more importantly, I needed to stop worrying and become more mindful. Remember, these were the days when I had no idea that this would become such a huge way of life for me.

My mind likes to work in pictures and cartoons, although I don't have the artistic skill to recreate any of them here. Thank heavens my lovely illustrator can see inside my brain! When my mind gets busy and starts to run away with itself, my thoughts form a type of flow chart.

In the early days of marriage things were quite difficult for us as a couple. My husband had sold his lovely cottage in the country to fund my new business, and we lived in the flat above. This flat was a dirty, dusty, dated, messy shell. We had no bathroom for weeks and floorboards with holes in them for months. It was by far much, much bigger than our little cottage, but we were now in the centre of town. There was noise. There was traffic. The flat needed total renovation, which my husband would do on weekends, after a trip down the M4 on a Friday afternoon and the reverse journey at 5:00 a.m. on a Monday morning. Whoever said the first year of marriage was wonderful didn't live in our household. It was strained and stressful. I had a team of staff, all women, and he was used to dealing with the military. As with all new businesses, we had teething problems, and there would always be staff issues, with some off sick, some on maternity leave, ongoing training, performance reviews, and other minor crises, such as who got the free parking spaces and who was paying for what at the Christmas party. My poor husband would get home after a week away and I would bombard him with 'stuff'—things we needed to do, things the girls had or hadn't done. And the flat was a bomb site! Not an easy transition time at all. When tensions ran high, my mind was a flow chart.

If they do this or say that, then I will do this. Then, if this happens, then I will do this…or even this. Then, if that happens, I will implement this. Then, if that happens, I could do this!

What scrambled thoughts in my head! No wonder I was stressed. What a waste of energy and time.

Now, if I could turn the clock back and see what sparked the argument in the first place, it was probably just a little thing one of us said. We were not being impeccable with our words, and the other maybe made an assumption. From there came an escalation of words you normally have in an argument—you know, the 'and another thing', or even the 'you said…!'

STOP! The key to this is to firstly *notice* what is happening. Notice how your thoughts are escalating and STOP.

Take a moment. Stop and breathe. Stop making assumptions about what the other is thinking. You are not a mind reader. You are not the other person. You are you. Take responsibility for our own actions.

If you are impeccable with your word, people cannot make assumptions, and if they end up doing just that, then that is their choice and their own perspective. If others are not impeccable with their words and are aggressive or callous

or mean, you have to be very strong and not take things personally. You have no idea what the other person's values and thoughts are. Trying to implement the 'not taking things personally' part of the four agreements is, I find, the most difficult. Sometimes words are said and not retracted. If those words hold value and are true, they may need a response. They may need to be given an apology. This is your choice. By standing back and just looking at the bigger picture, you can deflect things easily by not allowing someone else's beliefs or comments to affect you. If you have been impeccable with your word, you won't have people making comments that cause you to take things personally.

The last agreement of always doing your best, shouldn't really need an explanation, but if you always do your best even though it may not be as 'good' as you did yesterday, you are safe in the knowledge that you did as well as you could.

I've found that in recent years, these agreements come into play with the explosive use of social media. I only discovered social media a few years ago and embraced Twitter much more than Facebook. It was my choice, although I have a presence on both. It is very easy to take offence at someone's post on Facebook or at someone's tweet. The drama of a situation can easily fuel anger and get out of hand. People who post on group community sites can stir up feelings of anger as easily as feelings of support and generosity.

Recently we had a natural disaster in the UK with severe weather. Massive amounts of flooding in Somerset as well as Wales, Gloucester, and the Thames Valley. The coastline was being battered by Mother Nature doing her worst. A mixture of global warming, badly managed farmland, poor government policies, and lack of communication and facts from the environmental agencies all round led to a disaster in many places, with houses that have never flooded before being abandoned as floodwaters rose to over eight feet, with cars barely visible on the roads and farmers having to evacuate cattle in the hundreds. Wildlife was dying. Railway lines were ripped away from their foundations with gale-force winds, causing actual waves across the countryside that had never experienced anything so catastrophic.

Social media was either amazing and uplifting or condemning, depending on which posts you chose to read. I am no politician, and although I have lived in Somerset all my life, all the ins and outs of who was to blame for this disaster became quite a blur. Everyone had a different opinion on who was to blame. Everyone had a different perspective. All I could see was a sea of anger, rather than people pulling together and dealing with it. Naturally this was very traumatic for all concerned, and I have no doubt that having to leave your home must be the worst possible thing; it is your haven. I had great sadness for the wildlife that had been killed and the people who would be homeless for many months, some of whom were my friends.

At the beginning I started to share tweets about imminent weather warnings and road closures during the days of the worst weather. I could help by sharing posts on Facebook with people needing coordination to help evacuate animals and bring in food and sandbags. I saw the good in people and how fast social media could get a relief effort moving so quickly. Then it became apparent that there was much anger. On reading comments on posts that I saw as useful and good, I became saddened that people just wanted to blame others. I 'liked' a comment by someone who had mentioned that help was actually coming and being pledged though people were still moaning. I woke the next morning to an inbox message from someone who I didn't know, who had actually had nothing better to do than look at who had 'liked' the comment and messaged me to shout obscenities over how I could like such a post! Had she made assumptions as to why I had liked it? Was she so full of anger she was venting at anyone? Who knows her reasons, but the instant reaction I felt was anger too. I was upset and angry that someone could use words in that way, without thinking and without actually knowing me. Remember, I had not made a comment on this Facebook post; I had just clicked 'like' after someone else commented—not the main post. The main post was about help coming to those who needed it. Yet the resultant anger and resentment was immense.

From just a click, someone from a group set up to help people on Facebook was sparked to rant at me. Did this cause me distress? Maybe. I had to take a moment and be mindful. I had to check in and feel this emotion in my body. Then, when I was 'clear', I could decide what to do. Ignore it? Justify it? I was so upset that these words from someone I didn't know could hurt so much. They were just words, but hurtful, as the person who wrote them was making an assumption.

I chose to reply. What I replied with is of no consequence here, but in my reply I was impeccable with my word. What the recipient chose to do with that was up to her. She chose not to reply. The hardest part for me was not taking her comment personally, and this was a very difficult thing to do.

Let it go. Allowing emotions like this to fester will cause disharmony within your body, but feel it. Yes, you guessed it: *you are human, after all!*

I chose to go back and focus on all the amazing posts on Facebook about help being given and animal feed and pet supplies being shipped in convoys from all over the country. Farmers were giving all their help to others with tractors and trailers, moving sandbags, and the Dutch were arriving with massive pumps to help clear the waters away. I accepted that people felt anger; it was their choice, and I am sure that if I had been a little closer to the flooded areas, I would have been feeling that too, but I was still saddened that everyone was looking for someone to blame despite help being sent in very quickly—although not quickly enough for some. If you focused on the good, and by that I mean the good work that the communities were doing to get help in, rather than making assumptions as to why help wasn't being sent in by the government, then the dynamics would change.

We don't actually know all the ins and outs of why this and that didn't happen. People were demanding help and answers but were unaware of what was actually going on behind the scenes to get the help to them. Assumptions were being made and with good reason, but there has to be a point when you choose to stop blaming and decide to use the energy elsewhere.

It doesn't matter if you post a comment on a media site or speak directly to someone—be impeccable with your word and do what your elders taught you: think before you speak. If you just take a moment and think and are impeccable with your word, hopefully the words spoken cannot be taken out of context. In the grand scheme of the intricate weaving of the universe, if I hadn't clicked that 'like' button, chapter nine would not have been written with a personal experience relating directly to the modern ways of using your word.

YOGA MOJO

Love it, hate it, or never tried it, there is no denying that yoga has become incredibly popular in the last few years. There are so many types, so many teachers, and many companies selling yoga clothing, mats, and books. There are retreats focusing on yoga and meditation advertised in those eco-friendly yoga magazines, and every gym now offers a yoga class of some sort.

In my view yoga is something everyone should try. It has come a long way from being perceived as very bendy people tying themselves in knots while burning incense and chanting. The key is to give it a go, find a teacher that suits you, and don't give up after the first class.

My journey with yoga started when I was very young. My godmother was a bit of a yogi, and my early memories as a child were of cycling round to her house and finding her doing a headstand up the lounge wall in her petticoat. Strange, the things you remember when you start writing a book!

Way back at school, I was a lazy girl where exercise was concerned, and I hated all competitive sport. I could be found playing right or left back in hockey for the good side, so they were always at the other end scoring. I could stay nice and safe at the other end—cold and wet, but safe!

We were never really taught how to 'do' exercise. If a cross-country run were sprung upon us, the teachers were only interested in the leaders of the pack. The poor souls at the back of the pack, in their Dunlop daps, wheezed in just in time for the bell for the next lesson. It was harsh. The only PE class I didn't mind was 'popmobility', or, to use its modern name, aerobics. Back in the early '80s this was cutting-edge in schools, and one PE teacher, Mrs Vine, really pushed to get us all to try it! I was in heaven. No competition! I can even remember the music they used: "I Put My Blue Jeans On" by Keith Urban. I had no idea that one day I would be teaching classes like that myself.

In our O-level year we were offered a selection of sport—as if it were a treat! All I could do was look for the easiest option. We had to choose two to be split throughout the year. I opted for swimming and yoga! I couldn't believe it. Swimming meant you could walk to the local pool after lunch, spend the time bobbing about and chatting, and then go home straight from there. No need to return to base. This was superb. I can't actually remember much about the yoga classes except for some candle-gazing relaxation therapy, but I know that I enjoyed it much more than the other sports on the list!

When I was at college training in hairdressing and beauty therapy, a compulsory part of the course was 'exercise to music'. This was in the days of Jane Fonda and ankle warmers, just before shell suits and cheese-wire-bottomed leotards! We learnt how to teach aerobic classes. We spent hours counting beats to tracks of music by Madonna and Bananarama. We taught the rest of the class each week, and it was not competitive—just up my street. We had assignments to complete, and this led to a summer project being set to compare three different contrasting types of exercise. This was well before computers, so it was all researched and handwritten, with images traced from textbooks. It took all summer, but I chose swimming, weight training, and of course yoga.

Little was I to know then that our friend yoga was tapping me on the shoulder as early as my late teens, and would be a big part of my life later on. There was something there, something that really interested me, and when I left college it disappeared for a while when I started to teach aerobic classes. There would always be some stretch work at the end of my classes, but pure yoga was not something I was really interested in. It was actually too slow for me! I was busy building my business and had no time for such classes. This was, however, back in the 1980s, so styles like Vinyasa flow were not really available. It was all Hatha yoga with lots of meditation. Not for me, thank you very much. Not then, anyway.

Yoga was to pop up again when a friend of mine, Paula, was training to be a yoga teacher and needed a guinea pig to practice with. We used to meet in the gym, having done cardio work first, and then sneak into one of the studios for an hour to practice. Paula was developing her own class in Taunton, and I was lucky to be part of her practice, but sadly, living out of town made it difficult to finish clients early enough to get in through the traffic to participate in one of her actual classes, so I started home practice instead. I did what most people do when they haven't quite 'got it' yet. I studied books and magazines and wished I could do all the advanced poses. I never had any desire for headstands and scorpions, but a 'royal pigeon'? Now that sounded and looked rather spectacular.

It was about this time that I was beginning to use Twitter to network with other like-minded people, and I asked the question one day about yoga retreats.

I felt I needed some focus in my practice. The universe works in mysterious ways, and someone popped up out of the Twittersphere suggesting I follow @AnnSeeYeoh. Ann-See was just about to launch a workshop event in East Brent in North Somerset, which is only a half-hour

drive from me and was a perfect chance to learn and absorb more yoga. I did manage to meet Ann-See briefly before the event and instantly felt a connection—a real generous spirit with a passion for yoga and fitness, helped by the fact that she was my age, too!

The first workshop was full, and I mean *full,* of BodyPump instructors. They were incredibly upper body fit and had incredible stamina. They all knew Ann-See, and I felt I was out of my depth. I plonked myself down at the back of the class and hoped for the best. In the early days these workshops were run from more of a fitness perspective, as the participants, being mainly instructors, had only experienced yoga in a gym setting, and they didn't have much experience with the woo woo. As time has moved on, many of these first participants have fallen by the wayside and the dynamics of the class have changed. Each workshop now has a theme, and this enables you to grow and develop your yoga practice. Ann-See still runs these day workshops every two or three months, and I try to attend when I can, with only bad weather in the winter keeping me away.

I have learnt many new things and over the first year I gradually migrated towards the front of the class, as I had more confidence and needed to be able to see the instructor more easily. I soon became aware that it really doesn't matter what others are doing on their mats or how bendy they are; it only matters what you are doing and how you feel. If you are in the moment and focusing on your own practice, you don't actually see anyone else. It is useful, however, if you are new, to have someone in front of you that you can follow if you get lost—and you are of course human and allowed some sort of awe over those who can move effortlessly into positions that you can only dream of. The trick is acknowledging that you can be inspired and appreciate a beautiful Vinyasa flow in front of you, but that it's what you do on your own mat that matters. No one knows your body like you do. No one else can feel the movement; no one else can understand the depth of the breath you have just experienced.

However, I began to fall out of love with yoga and lost my yoga mojo about eighteen months before writing this book. I had started

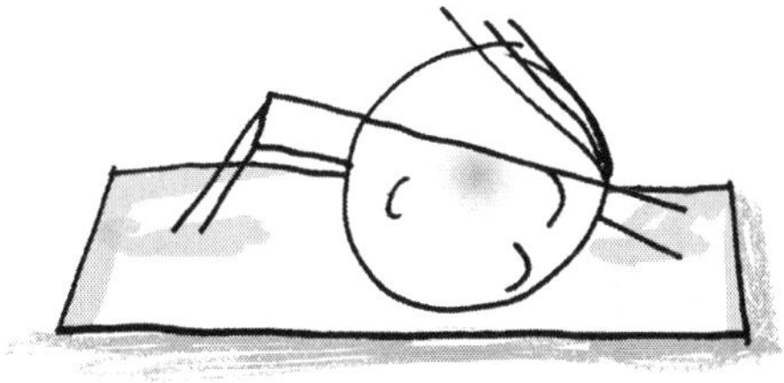

attending Paula's weekly evening class by carving out time in my day so I could get into town in plenty of time and not arrive frazzled. It was lovely being part of a group, and occasionally I would stay and do the second class, which was more intensive. I had no interest in mastering the headstand or the wheel and would listen to my body and stop when I needed to. Some of the arm balances I found tricky too, having broken my wrist in the past. I knew my limits.

At one of Ann-See's workshops, we were practicing the crow pose. Everyone made it look so effortless, and I must have been doing something wrong! I just couldn't 'get it'. Were my arms not strong enough? Was my centre of gravity off kilter? I was so frustrated. When arrived home, I discovered even my husband could do it! So I decided to practice—a lot! I injured myself. I overstretched my sacroiliac joint, and I was so angry with myself. I realised that

I was trying too hard and should have taken some one-to-one instruction. I had also been using the momentum of movements to get through the flow, rather than using my core. I had been performing the sun salutation incorrectly for years and had caused all sorts of problems with my lower back. I didn't know; it had looked okay! I thought yoga had caused the injury, and I became afraid of trying it again. My love for yoga was disappearing. Then I had a lightbulb moment—well, a few little ones put together, actually!

I had missed some workshops during the winter, and my yoga mojo took a while to return. After a day with Ann-See, enabling me to reconnect with the essence of my practice and not be frustrated that I'd had an injury, I found my love of yoga again. I had got so caught up in the drama of *why* I was injured and what pose had done this to me that I had become disillusioned with all yoga. I needed to take a step back and get down to basics—to be kind to myself and focus on the needs of my body, and not on what I used to be doing. I needed to be in the moment. And I realised that even the tutor had back issues, and indeed many other people in the class had some kind of specific ailment and stiffness. Yoga will move with you. If you are injured, sad, happy, energetic, or just needing some TLC, yoga can do so much. Just listen, breathe, and notice.

It's not all about the shape of the pose. It's about how you feel in the pose.

Every body is different.

Every time you approach your mat, you will feel different, and your practice with reflect this.

Every teacher is different.

Yoga is an old practice. According to Wikipedia, yoga is the physical, mental, and spiritual practices or disciplines which aim at transforming body and mind. The term denotes a variety of schools, practices, and goals in Hinduism, Buddhism, and Jainism, the best known being Hatha yoga. The origins date back hundreds of years, and Hatha yoga emerged at the turn of the first millennium. Gurus from India introduced yoga to the Western world, and in the late nineteenth century yoga became more of a physical exercise throughout the West. Since the 1980s there have been many 'new' types of yoga emerging to fit in to our lifestyles, but all have their roots within Hatha yoga. If you are a newcomer, try a Hatha-based class first so you can become familiar with the postures.

When someone says to you, 'Oh, I do yoga', remember they may not do yours. When someone 'gets' yoga, he or she will have discovered how the breath is so important, and understood the essence behind the moves. There is no need to learn the Sanskrit names or to wear the latest trendy clothing. Just be mindful on your mat. Be present to how your body feels and use your breath. Remember chapter four? Everyone will have a different natural breath length. Find yours and use it. Use your mindfulness skill and be aware.

Top Tips!

- Ask friends about different classes and teachers, and find a class that suits your time scale. There is no point turning up having ploughed through the traffic in a hot and bothered state, unable to catch your breath, just as the rest of the class is settling in for the start. Plan to arrive ten minutes early so you can settle on your mat.

- Ask the tutor if you can try a class first before committing to a course. Most teachers will be only too pleased to do this for you. Ensure that they ask you about any medical issues you may have. If they don't, then leave them well alone. Equally, if you are a regular in a class, it is wise to inform your tutor if you have any injury.

- I would also suggest that you invest in your own mat. I cannot understand why someone would want to use a mat provided by the gym or dance space, knowing that they are going to lie on it with their face resting where someone else's perspiring feet may have been! I like a fabric mat, but many prefer one that has more 'stick' to it so they can hold positions with more stability. If you are going to progress to Ashtanga yoga, you will need a mat on which you can slide from one posture to another. Sticky mats don't work as well for that type of yoga. Think about the manufacturing of your mat and how eco-friendly it is, too. You will spend a long time on it. Choose wisely.

- Hydrate well, as with all exercise. Just because you aren't moving very fast doesn't mean that your body can get through the session without water. The more hydrated your body is, the more easily energy will flow. And try not to perform yoga within at least two hours of eating.

- Remove jangly jewellery, as this can be distracting, and choose clothing that stays put. There is nothing worse than having to readjust your clothing so things don't ride up—or down! Layers are a good idea.

- Phones to silent! It goes without saying.

- Listen to your body. If you are finding it difficult to maintain a pose, come out of it. Injuries happen when you push the boundaries a little too far—usually because you are watching someone else in what you believe to be a deeper stretch.

- Watch others in the class if you need to check you are facing the right way, but listen to your own body. I learnt there is a difference between being in awe of someone else and getting annoyed that you can't do the same, and being aware of someone else's ability but knowing that everyone else is different. Remember, some people will have been practicing yoga for much longer than you, and in many cases the outstanding ones will be gymnast trained. So don't beat yourself up about it.

- Try not to leave before Savasana—the relaxation part at the end. It completes the practice and allows you to take a moment and reconnect before leaving the studio. It is seen as bad manners if you leave before the end of a class. If you know in advance that you need to sneak out before the end, position yourself near the exit and tell the instructor at the start. Be respectful of others and leave quietly.

Below is a list of the most widely known yoga styles, to help you understand more.

Hatha

Hatha basically refers to any type of yoga that teaches physical postures. Most people will have attended a Hatha yoga class, especially in the West. It gives you a perfect grounding, although you won't work up a sweat in one of these classes. It gives you focus and in my view is a very pure form of yoga. You should end up leaving a class feeling more stretched and relaxed.

Vinyasa Flow

Vinyasa (pronounced "vin-yah-sah") is the Sanskrit word for 'flow'. Vinyasa classes are based on a sequence of movements that can be quite intensive. Movements are choreographed and classes smoothly transition from pose to pose, giving perfect balance with controlled breathing techniques. The intensity of the practice is similar to Ashtanga, but no two Vinyasa classes are the same, as the tutor will choreograph their own sequence. If you like to feel you have worked out, this is a superb class.

Ashtanga

Based on ancient yoga teachings, this style of yoga was brought to the West by Pattabhi Jois in the 1970s. It's a rigorous style of yoga that follows a specific sequence of postures and is similar to Vinyasa yoga, using linked breath. It is always performed with the exact same poses in the exact same order. If you attend one class, you will find the same routine in another. It is a very demanding practice and often a teacher will only allow you to progress through the whole series of movements once you have mastered the previous section correctly. This is a hot, physically demanding practice.

Bikram

Bikram Choudhury developed this school of yoga about thirty years ago, so it is relatively new. Classes are held in artificially superheated rooms, where you will sweat like you've never sweated before. You work your way through a series of twenty-six poses, a little like in an Ashtanga class. These classes can only be called Bikram if the routine is kept exact, as it has been trademarked. If a class is called 'hot yoga' it will be similar, but will not be these exact movements. These classes are becoming very popular with those wanting more of a workout.

Iyengar

This form of yoga was developed by B. K. S. Iyengar and is a very precise style. Attention is given to finding the proper alignment in a pose, using an assortment of props such as blocks, straps, and bolsters. There isn't a lot of jumping around in Iyengar classes, like there is with Ashtanga, so you won't develop much perspiration, but you will discover how physically and mentally challenging it is to stay in one pose.

Personally, I prefer Vinyasa classes, as I enjoy the flow and the use of breath. I haven't tried Bikram, and I like to be able to do my yoga anywhere I can, so Iyengar doesn't work for me either, as I don't like to work with props.

I am a firm believer in one-to-one yoga classes. If you can afford it, and it is money well spent, go to a few classes first, and then book a personal session. Very often with one-hour group classes, the teachers are restricted to how much adjustment they can give you due to the time constraints and the need to keep an eye on everyone else. With a one-to-one session, time can be spent showing you the importance of the breath while working with the poses and flow that *your* body needs. This is a huge bonus and often changes your perception of yoga completely.

Your kind of yoga could be gentle or challengingly hot or very bendy. Whatever yoga works for you, it enables you to be focused and become present. Through it you will understand how your body moves and feels and how to create a connectedness with the subtle energies of the universe.

Yoga is focus. Yoga is breath. Yoga rocks.

Mindfulness on Your Mat

Having hosted many mindfulness events over the past few years, I have seen a great cross section of participants. Some arrive knowing nothing about the subject and were coerced into attending, while others have more grounding in the woo woo but would just like a nice day out to hear the teachings of someone else. These workshop days have made me more aware of how different healing modalities and lifestyles overlap, and one of the concepts that always unites people is yoga.

Many of the attendees will have tried yoga at some point in their lives, and they have stories about the type that they prefer or how difficult they found it. After a day of mindfulness, when they begin to realise that everything revolves round the breath, they can see that yoga is all about being mindful. Some may never have been shown this in a class, and when you 'get it', it can be quite amazing!

The mindfulness of the breath is so important. When you approach your mat in a focused way and bring your attention to your breath, you will be truly in the moment, able to focus on your practice in a different way. It's not all about the stretch. It's about being aware of your body and how it feels.

Bringing mindfulness to your mat is so logical.

It brings you to your breath, and your breath enables you to become present.

You should now begin to see how all previous chapters are overlapping, and with breath work, mindfulness, and manifesting, you will realise how many things are so beautifully interwoven into our lives. So many people will never want to try any of these amazing things, while others will discover yoga in their 'middle age' and totally embrace it. Some will have already learnt how to meditate, and others will have been vegetarian from a very young age.

We are in an amazing, liberating time in our universe, and for those of us who understand how everything on the planet is connected, it is with immense gratitude that I am happy to be alive now, and to be enjoying the process of humanity waking up a bit!

WHERE'S THE JUICE?

The title for this chapter was 'given' to me after a yoga class in Taunton one Saturday afternoon. I rarely get to go this quite powerful class, as I'm normally working, but I had decided to take a day off on this day, as the following day I was taking a fully attended mindfulness workshop at the Langford Hotel, out on the Somerset Levels. Having the day off prior to an event like that has proved a good call, allowing me to attend a class with different people and different dynamics. Normally it was a treat, but today I was unable to partake due to being a little 'broken' in the hip/ lower back region. I had been advised by my osteopath to stay away from yoga until my treatment had unraveled me a little more. I therefore spent an hour in a coffee shop reading a yoga magazine, which, in my view, was the next best thing.

I did, however, make time for the lunch and chat with the group afterwards. The sun shone and the company was, as always, inspiring. Seven yogis around a table is always an interesting combination of energies. With the intricate workings of the universe and the subject of pathways and journeys being discussed, the book-writing saga was also brought into the mix. Someone who I have never had direct contact with, but whose face I knew from the class, was chatting with me about what I actually 'did'. As a business owner, I never leave the house without cards, and this time I had coloured fliers for my mindfulness events. Never pass up on a networking opportunity! Seeds were sown and the book writing was then discussed. How many chapters? What was left to do, and how many words had I already written?

When I started writing this, I had ten chapters in my mind. No real structure, but ten chapters with a few certainties, and with the others to 'flow' as the book evolved. The last one was going to be about my journey with yoga, but I had missed another important topic: nutrition. Without writing a science-based list of nutrients and their use in the body, and without lecturing people on why they should or shouldn't eat raw, or go vegetarian, I wanted to write about nourishment of the body. I had also forgotten that one of the big subjects I tweet about is juicing. I had missed this completely, and this newfound yogi friend said, 'Oh no! Where's the juice?!'

So this chapter was born, and the eleventh chapter you now have.

I am not a nutritionist. I did not go to university and study nutrition, but back in the day it was a big part of my beauty-therapy training, and thankfully, when I was at school food and nutrition was an O-level subject. I have always been fascinated with how different foods affected the body and which foods went well with others in the cooking process. I had always been interested in preparing balanced meals, and I like to think I am a good cook. In fact, schoolteachers had no interest in helping me pursue my career as a beauty therapist. They wanted me to go into catering. I defied them and took my own pathway, and now to some extent I can combine the two together.

As we have evolved over the past thirty years, different diets have come and gone. There was the cabbage soup diet, the pineapple diet, the Beverly Hills diet. My mother used Weight Watchers, and then, in the mid eighties, Slimming World was born. We have had low-carb, low-fat, and fat-free diets, the Atkins and Cambridge diets, the 5:2 diet, and on and on. Diet, diet, diet. Everyone is so wound up with choosing which diet to lose weight that they often fail to see that if health came before weight loss, their weight wouldn't be so much of an issue.

In my view, education in basic nutrition is lacking, with most teenagers these days thinking that cooking is piercing film tops on plastic trays and throwing them in

the microwave. Getting the population to understand what they are actually eating is quite difficult, as we have evolved to the point of grabbing a sandwich and a diet drink on the run. We have become people who want things faster and easier. I remember as a child when Pot Noodles were created, and it was so exciting! Instant noodles by just adding boiling water—this was amazing! We had no idea exactly what we were eating. No interest in the chemicals and the lack of actual nutrition. The instant food industry was growing fast! Microwaves were no longer an elite kitchen appliance. Every kitchen soon had one, and instant 'cooking' became the norm.

As students in the 1980s, we didn't have much money, and our diets could have been a lot better than they were, despite taking nutrition as part of the course. As a student you rarely practiced what you learnt, because you couldn't. Those faddy diets were of great interest to beauty therapy students. We too wanted to be thin. Tablets, shakes—all from a bottle or a sachet.

My mother and stepfather had a dairy farm, which meant at weekends when I was home from college I drank the most glorious unpasteurised milk skimmed directly from the top of the tank. My mother bought nice food for me to eat, which included lovely cheeses. Unknown to me, after consuming all this high dairy food I developed an intolerance in the form of eczema and sluggish digestion. I developed a congested complexion despite using a professional brand of products.

In those days you used to treat the skin by using topical preparations, and back in the '80s there were a lot less skin care ranges than there are now. Organic brands were relatively unheard of, and Clarins was the widest-used salon brand. Clinique was what most non-salon visiting women would opt for if they had a skin problem, as it was available in department stores and sold by white-coated, medical-looking consultants. For a consumer there wasn't really much to choose from.

My first ever salon was very quiet, and I spent a lot of time running myself ragged trying to work after-hours by treating friends and nursing home residents to make enough money to put fuel in the car to get to work the next day. It wasn't easy, and

I became quite run down. If this had happened now, I would have a completely different outlook, and there would be more available to me to get me through the stress on my body and my mind: mindfulness, yoga, and most importantly, nutrition! Well, to be honest, I wouldn't allow this situation to happen to me now. I have more knowledge, and I have evolved into being more food savvy.

One of the most effective ways to cleanse and tonify the liver is to try juicing. In recent years this has become a big part of my daily routine. If only I had had all the knowledge and information I have now back then, I would have been a lot healthier—but then I wouldn't have such a story to tell. Instead I drank hot chocolate and ate millionaire's shortbread on a daily basis to cheer myself up. This in turn fed my digestive issues and created more eczema. It wasn't until I was referred by my GP to the hospital for an allergy test that I discovered I had an intolerance to dairy and artificial colours.

I stopped eating all dairy, and in those days this was quite difficult, as dairy alternatives were not readily available. No almond, rice, or hazelnut milk, and no soya margarines in supermarkets. The only substitute was something called 'granose' that you could get only from health-food shops. The soya milk tasted musty and the margarine was very bland. I didn't eat dairy for months and my skin improved, but I had developed IBS. Well, in those days, if you had it, you didn't know what it was, and doctors didn't really have a solution for it, other than giving you a delightful product called fibre gel. It was a client who recommended that I see her herbalist—expensive, unusual, and I had to travel to find her.

She used iridology to help diagnose what was wrong, and gave me some quite disgusting tonic to drink. The most powerful information I came away with was the following:

Brew your tea. I used to drink what I called 'quick tea' made by having the first cup from the pot before it had a chance to brew. I was drinking it black due to lack of dairy, and allowing the tea to brew made it way too strong. It was explained to me that tannin is released first when the boiling water hits the tea, and this is acidic. It then takes five minutes for the caffeine to be released. The caffeine then neutralises the acid.

With the advent of one-cup tea bags, the brewing of tea has become a thing of the past. A quick dunk for most people to get a decent colour, usually drunk first thing in the morning, as we are British and like our tea, and all you are doing is drinking acid. Lovely.

Obviously this isn't the same for herbal teas, but even those should be brewed to ensure all the nutrients are released.

Take your time. The best way to have black tea is to brew it correctly with more water than normal if it's just for you, or to add hot water to your cup when everyone else is adding their milk. Use a teapot. That's why they were invented.

White bread and jam is a very bad combination.

I used to eat a lot of white bread, especially at the time of the month when I couldn't eat chocolate due to my intolerance to dairy—this was before the introduction of Green & Blacks', and way before raw chocolate was even heard of. To sweeten the bread, I used to cover it in raspberry jam. Delicious! It certainly sorted out my craving for sweet things. What it 'gave' me in return was Candida. A continual monthly cycle followed every period, and I was plagued for years. All the GP could offer was Canesten, and I had this on a continual repeat prescription. No advice at all. Just something to help the symptoms.

It was this brilliant herbalist who told me the sugar in the jam was combining with the yeast in the bread even before my saliva could work on it, and yeast was forming in excess. This was causing an explosion of Candida in my gut every month. And there I was thinking I was being really 'good' staying away from dairy and chocolate. What an eye opener this was. So logical and even so, my GP had no interest in this at all.

I stopped this cycle and cured my Candida, and also in turn cured my eczema, which had got quite out of control on my forehead, neck, and wrists. Such a roundabout way, and quite a journey to get there, but what now seems so simple was actually difficult to grasp in those days.

Many years have passed since then, and I can now tolerate a little dairy, so a well-made ice cream, not one filled with additives, or a lovely hot chocolate on the mountain while skiing does not cause my eczema to flare up. I do however find these foods quite rich now and prefer to make smoothies with almond milk, and I rarely have ice cream.

With age, rosacea tends to appear on the face, and with me, my nose now has a tendency to develop red bumps if I eat strawberries or tomatoes (known 'sensitisers'). Alcohol also has the same effect, but I very rarely drink now, having stopped several years ago. My aversion to wine was triggered by my taste buds changing when I started teaching more Reiki. If I do partake in an occasional glass of red, my nose is a little dotted the next day, just like someone has taken a felt-tip pen to it.

With any sensitivity, it's all about realising that you have it. Many people have no idea which foods suit them, and others are actually so 'toxic' from processed foods that they have become addicted to the chemicals and sugars and have no idea what real fresh food actually is. Part of this is due to poor education at school level and parents not being able to teach children to cook. The other part is the fact that fast food and microwavable dinners are affordable. The fast food industry is massive, while the organic food industry is more expensive and more difficult to find. Thankfully things are slowly changing due to media coverage of the way foods are made, and TV chefs like Jamie Oliver exposing subjects like school dinners for what they are and actually getting the government to make changes. The sad thing is that the situation shouldn't have been allowed to get out of hand in the first place, but being mindful, we must be thankful that now things are changing!

One of the most recent food trends is juicing. I don't really like calling it a trend, as it's not at all like the faddy diets people follow. Juicing can be used as a detox and can also be added to your daily routine to ensure you are getting top-quality fruits and vegetables straight into your system. It's more like a lifestyle change rather than a 'fad', and I love it! It was my yoga teacher, Ann-See Yeoh that told me about it a few years ago. She was promoting the idea of alkalinity within the body and juicing more green vegetables than fruit. She recommended a juicer and I dutifully ordered it. When it arrived, in the box was a book on juicing by Jason Vale. I had no idea who this man was, and after a little research, I soon discovered that he was the face of juicing in the UK and had written many books. Since then he has become a very powerful advocate via social media for juicing, and he has opened his stunning Juicy Oasis Retreat in Portugal. He leads a global detox at various times during the year and has recently made a documentary called *Super Juice Me*, which was an inspiration. It's not all about weight loss, but about general health. It's about understanding what your body needs and allowing it to heal.

Jason has his own powerful story that is an inspiration to many. My persistent chatter on Twitter has helped many people see how this little addition to their lifestyle can help them attain their five a day (or even seven or ten a day, as is now being suggested). Sometimes clients arrive having been inspired to do a full five-day detox, feeling full of beans with glowing skin and a spring in their step. They then continue with a healthier eating plan and a daily juice. It's perfect.

For me, a morning green juice to ensure alkalinity within the body is a must. Apparently the more alkali the body is, the more it is able to keep cancer cells at bay. There are many books on the market about the 'pH diet'.

Sometimes I make a beetroot-based juice to help with sports performance if my husband is going to play golf. It is known that Olympian athletes drink beetroot juice to help with oxygenation of the blood. I also like to use ginger and turmeric in my juices to warm the digestion and help maintain healthy joints. Be aware that you will need to add a fruit to the beetroot, or it will be very bitter. Ideal blends are apple, cucumber, and beetroot with a slice of lemon and a small piece of ginger, or, apple, carrot, parsnip, and beetroot, lovely in the winter.

Juicing Tips

- Juicing is not the same as making a smoothie. Smoothies are blended usually with milk or yoghurt, or sometimes a green juice can be added to the blender with avocado or banana to thicken and add fibre.

- There are many juicers on the market. Unless you are juicing all day every day for a family of ten, you really don't need to spend a fortune on one. The juicers these days are so easy to clean, with little waste produced. I use a centrifugal one that cost about eighty pounds. There are 'masticating' ones which use more of the fruit and veggies, but they take longer to process and often cost more. Ensure it is strong enough to take beetroot and ensure that whole apples will fit through the chute. The older versions required much peeling and chopping! It is personal choice, but aim to spend between sixty and one hundred pounds. Mine is still going strong after three years of daily juicing.

- More vegetables and less fruit. Keep your sugar levels down.

- You will get through a lot of apples. These form the base to most juices.

- You will get fibre in the form of soluble pectin from apples, but when you transfer to your blender and add avocado, that will give you a bulkier juice and even more fibre.

- Drink your juices mindfully. Allow the vitamins to fill your body. If you are doing a full detox, take your time and savour the taste and texture.

- If you choose to do a full detox, plan your time well. It's not really advisable to take on a full five-day detox if you are working flat-out, especially for the first three days, when you can feel a little lethargic as your body adjusts to any changes—especially due to a sudden lack of caffeine!

- Following a juice detox programme to the letter will give you focus, but remember to listen to your body. There may be things you really can't stomach. So change it. I'm not keen on celery. One stick in with many other ingredients is fine, but more than that, and I would turn it down!

- Pack your smaller leafy items, like spinach, in between other vegetables. Squash them down in the chute with your lemon slice and ginger. It stops it spinning straight out the other side. And remember, you can juice the stalks of broccoli—no wastage!

- If you are not a cook and find it difficult to decide which vegetables will work together without making a brown, foul-tasting sludge, have a look at Jason Vale's website for juicing recipes. There is now an app and a good selection of books, too.

As we become more aware and more mindful, we should be able to be understand the needs of our body and how food can affect our mood and our digestion. This is all part of the 'waking up' process and the journey to woo woo land! I could write chapters on the benefits of eating 'clean' and knowing where your food comes from. I could discuss the need to get back to how the food industry was in the old days, and of the need to stop the mass farming, which isn't helping the planet at all. I didn't want this book to be too controversial, and I wanted it to be an easy read, so I will leave that subject well alone.

All I will say is just think about what you are eating. Mass-produced food from plastic packets that has been sprayed with pesticides can't be good for you. It is your choice whether you are vegan, vegetarian, wheat-free, or dairy-free. Some people will need to take an exclusion diet to help various health issues, while others will have moral reasons for omitting certain things from their diet. Everyone has a choice, and it is not for me to tell you what to eat, but just think about where your food comes from. So many people are now growing their own vegetables, and restaurants are taking to stating the providence of the food on their menu. We are slowly getting there. As with anything, it often takes the world to run away in one direction before we realise that we actually need to be doing something else.

Thinking of journeys and pathways on a massive scale, let's focus on the positive and give less energy to the politics that often underlie issues like this. I am no politician, but I too can easily get swept up in the social-media frenzy about mass farming and GM crops. I would rather focus on the writing about juicing and helping people notice the benefits of 'real' food. There is not much point in discussing the 'what if' and 'we shouldn't have' issues. Farming developed to a massive scale to feed us after the war, and processed foods were a complete breakthrough for busy households and still do have their place in our society. I like to think we have evolved enough to be able to make an informed choice about what we eat and how we eat.

To sum up.

Eat the best you can afford.

Read labels. If you don't recognise it, don't eat it.

Cook. It is never too late to learn how to cook your own food.

Eat clean.

Shop more often so your food stays fresh in the fridge.

Try juicing.

Eat less meat.

Be mindful when you eat. Remember chapter four.

And often an overlooked subject—drink more water!

As a therapist I am always telling clients to drink plenty of water. I even have a little statement now on the consultation cards they fill in to explain that after a treatment they need to hydrate well. It almost becomes almost a little mantra: 'Drink more water!' How much is 'more' though? Why should you drink it?

Well, there is much science involved in this answer—information about ionic exchange within your cells and the 'dehydration response'.

In basic terms, as humans we are made up of around 60 percent water, and we need to hydrate throughout the day. If you actually feel thirsty, you are already dehydrated deep within your body, and your liver is crying out for some water. The body has a superbly balanced system for excreting rubbish and being able to 'tick over' naturally, but we need to fuel it and hydrate it. Cells need moisture to enable the body to maintain its pH balance.

As the day moves into night, the cells become more acidic, making you more tired. During the night the more 'toxic' ions within the cells should naturally migrate out from within the cell, leaving you refreshed and ready for your day ahead, but if you are dehydrated you will wake feeling sluggish and not wanting to leap out of bed with great gusto! You are feeling this way because you are actually holding on to ions that need to move out of your cells, but can't due to lack of fluids.

Sodium and calcium are normally found outside the cell in the extracellular fluid. When we are active during the day, these ions move across the cell membrane and swap places with potassium and magnesium. During the resting nighttime, the moon naturally has an affinity with sodium and draws it together with the calcium out of the cell membrane, and potassium and magnesium move back in. This should be a perfect dance of electrolytes—that is, a perfect dance, as long as you are hydrated. If not, your cells produce a security band of cholesterol round themselves, protecting themselves from moisture loss. The body always works to protect us, and that is what it does: it protects the cell by reducing the permeability and therefore hindering the movement of electrolytes.

The solution is to drink more water, but how much is 'more'? This really does depend on the temperature of the day, how much exercise you are doing, and what altitude you are at. The general rule is two litres a day for women and three for men. That is not a litre of tea or coffee, as these will cause more urination due to caffeine and therefore cause more dehydration.

Take your water at room temperature so it doesn't shock your digestive system. Water in the form of herbal teas is acceptable and more agreeable during wintertime, when we trend to reach for those hot chocolates! Try herbal teas rather than fruit teas, which can be quite acidic, and try to drink most of your fluids by 6:00 p.m., as they say that is when the cellular exchange has already begun. One of the best starts to the day is the good old staple of hot water and lemon—a warming cleanse to the system, alkalising and hydrating. I like to add some ginger to kick-start the digestive system.

You can 'over drink', but this is not something you should be greatly concerned about, as to over drink and cause a serious imbalance in your kidneys would mean drinking so much that the electrolyte balance is seriously diluted. If you stick to your two litres a day and drink throughout the day rather than all in one go, you will be fine!

When we look at the need for water in more detail, we realise that the 'energy' within the cells of the body can move more easily when you are hydrated. The more hydrated you are, the more your body holds light. Light is energy. Energy is light. This is why, when you have received a healing therapy, massage, or such like, you will feel the need to urinate more due to the stimulation of the lymphatic system. This can lead to dehydration and subsequent headaches. Clients that say, 'That massage gave me a headache!' are probably correct, but they wouldn't have got one if they had hydrated. Healing requires hydration. The fastest way to address a sluggish body is to check the amount of water being drunk. Very often those clients who are always tired, have headaches, and never feel bright-eyed and bushy-tailed are just plain dehydrated. And when asked, 'How much water do you drink?' they often answer, 'Errr, not enough!'

As the body holds light and light is energy, energy needs water to flow. The more hydrated you are, the more connected you will be. Meditation and breath work will be much easier, and your digestion will improve. Your journey to woo woo land will be so much easier if you are bright-eyed and bushy-tailed.

Hydrate. Simple.

ARE WE THERE YET?

The title for this book came to me quite late in the writing process. I think it was at least chapter nine or even ten by the time it did literally 'come to me'. The title wasn't there at the concept, and I wasn't able to sit down and write continually over a few months, as I have my clients to treat and a house to run, so the whole process from start to finish has taken about ten months. As I wrote, the more everything fell into place, and as I said in the very first chapter, this book wasn't consciously channeled, but I did begin to understand why you have to write when you are in the mood, or when some defining event inspires you.

The title eluded me, though. People kept asking for it and I had absolutely no idea what to say. Then one day a new client arrived for healing. I just knew that she was with me for a reason other than just a treatment. I decided in my head to 'ask' during the treatment if there was anything I should know. This was new to me as a healer, as I normally go with the flow and don't get tied up in the drama of someone's story. I just 'do it'.

This was a defining moment. The answer came. Not through a voice telling me, but through me just 'getting it' in my head. Sometimes you have to stop trying so hard and *trust.*

Journey to Woo Woo Land.

As clear as day. It would have been unprofessional for me to whoop or jump up and down during a treatment, so I logged it in my mind and waited. I was so excited! I knew it was right. It was

right because sometimes people can be a bit woo woo, but you really don't need to be happy clappy to get the bigger picture. We are all human, we are all connected, and we all have a place on this planet.

This book will have given you a little insight into the things that will enable you to feel that connection and live your life with a little more ease and a little less stress. Using mindfulness and manifesting, you will discover easy tools to enable you to create wonderful things and lose the irrelevant chitter-chatter that just clogs up your thinking brain and blocks you from being free. Perhaps you will try some yoga and think a little more about breath work and the quality of the food you eat. I hope that you will be able to look out for signposts and realise that you don't have to do anything you don't want to do—but equally, try not to beat yourself up if you think you have taken the wrong path. There is no such thing as right or wrong. You just didn't like the route you took, so find another signpost. Look out for the signs and notice the light bulbs.

One of the biggest things I have learnt in my own journey is that everyone is different. This is what makes such a colourful human race, and no matter how excited you are about your new discoveries, you can't change the world and convert everyone all at once. You can only suggest, settle back, and watch. A little like sowing a seed. Watch it grow. You don't sow a seed and then dig it up to see if it has gained roots. Just allow it to develop by feeding and nurturing it. Your life will become more colourful when you are able to live in the moment. Remember, we need to make plans, but a plan is a basis for change, and you can change at any point.

This is your life and it is relatively short. Enjoy it. Do what fills you with joy.

So, are we there yet? Well, I truly believe you will really ever know what it is all about until you are no longer walking in a physical body. We hear stories, we can dream, but until that day comes, we will never really know what the bigger picture is. Treat your body well, take time out, recognise your stress triggers, and enjoy your life as it is now. Nourish yourself with energy-giving food and hydrate. You are energy. You are light.

Gain Present-moment awareness.

There is no such thing as a coincidence.

Everything is exactly as it should be.

Remember that.

BIBLIOGRAPHY

Byrne, Rhonda. *The Secret.*

Ellis, Richard. *Reiki and the Seven Chakras.*

Hay, Louisa L. *You Can Heal Your Life.*

Kabat-Zinn, Jon. *Mindfulness Meditation for Everyday Life.*

Ruiz, Don Miguel. *The Four Agreements.*

Walsh, Neal Donald. *Conversations with God.*

Williams, Mark and Danny Pearson. 2011. *Mindfulness: Finding Peace in a Frantic World.*

Wrenn, Barbara. *Cellular Awakening*

Nicki Hughes is just an ordinary girl finding her way towards the understanding that we are all connected. This book enables those who would like to know more about the 'woo woo' side of life to understand that it really is very simple. No need for complicated text and hours of meditation, incense burning, and mantras.

Journeys, pathways, and lightbulb moments are waiting for everyone if we just look for them and trust. Life is relatively short, so embrace it.

Everything happens for a reason. The synchronicity of the universe is a powerful thing and is there for everyone to see. You just have to notice. Open your eyes, heart, and soul.

Nicki can be found at www.waysidehouse.co.uk and @waysidehealer on Twitter.

8750769R00116

Printed in Great Britain
by Amazon.co.uk, Ltd.,
Marston Gate.